The Demons Of Athens

Reports From The Great Devastation

Vrasidas Karalis

16
EasyRead Large

RHYW

Copyright Page from the Original Book

Author's photo by András Berkes-Brandl

First published by Brandl & Schlesinger in 2014
PO Box 127 Blackheath NSW 2785 Australia
www.brandl.com.au

Australia Council for the Arts

This project has been assisted by the Australian Government through the Australia Council, its arts funding and advisory body.

Book design by András Berkes-Brandl

National Library of Australia Cataloguing-in-Publication entry:
Karalis, Vrasidas, author.
Title: The Demons of Athens / Vrasidas Karalis.
ISBN: 9781921556418 (paperback)
ISBN: 9781921556784 (epdf)
ISBN: 9781921556791 (epub/Kindle)
Subjects: Financial crises - Greece - 21st century. Athens (Greece) - Social conditions - 21st century. Greece - Social conditions - 21st century. Greece - Economic conditions - 21st century.
Dewey Number: 330.9495

VRASIDAS KARALIS

The Demons of Athens
Reports from the Great Devastation

VRASIDAS KARALIS is Professor of Modern Greek Studies at the University of Sydney. For the last 20 years, his area of research has been in Modern Greek, Byzantine, Cultural Studies and more recently Film Studies. He has published studies on Nikos Kazantzakis and Dionysios Solomos. He has translated two novels by the Australian Nobel Laureate Patrick White into Greek (*Voss, The Vivisector)* . He received the Federation Medal from the Federal Government in 2003. His recent publications include *Recollections of Mr Manoly Lascaris* (Brandl & Schlesinger), *Martin Heidegger and the Aesthetics of Living* (Cambridge Scholars) *Power, Judgement and Political Evil: In Conversation with Hannah Arendt* (Ashgate), *A History of Greek Cinema* (Continuum), and *Cornelius Castoriadis and the project of Radical Democracy* (Brill).

Also by Vrasidas Karalis

Martin Heidegger and the Aesthetics of Living
Recollections of Mr Manoly Lascaris
A History of Greek Cinema

NOTE

All incidents described in the following pages are actual events which took place between September 2011 and January 2013 in Athens. For some strange reasons of synchronicity the narrator was an eyewitness to most of them: the burning of the cinema, the destruction of computers at the university, the Muslim protests, the Ashura, the episode of the receipts on the island, the incident with the Neo-Nazis, the bomb at the shopping mall, and many more.

The fact that they were his personal experiences accounts for the autobiographical thread which weaves them into a continuous narrative.

Despite their chronological separation, they were put together for reasons of dramatic economy, as symbols of the atmosphere of urgency, tension and anxiety that dominates Athenian social life since the great contraction began in late 2009. The identity of certain public figures can easily be recognised; the identity of one or two interlocutors is better to remain concealed.

The current crisis has foregrounded the worst elements in the Greek political order: this story is about the entrapment of a nation by its political leadership. It is also about how people struggle to defend their existence from the semantic and moral nihilism that unfreedom has instituted as everyday reality.

I would like to thank Professor Anthony Stephens for his care over the shaping of the text and its stylistic excesses.

To Marie Meader, who left so gracefully

Day 1

Call me whatever you like, a deserter, a traitor, a drifter; but I must write down what I saw. It's an illuminating exercise: breaking away from the topographies of your beginning. Without narcissism or hubris: re-tracking and re-enacting. I hope you'll understand.

'Australian passport?' asks the police officer. I smile. Without even looking, he adds:

'I wish I could move to Australia; lots of money there. Here, nothing! We are all broke.'

I notice his Cartier watch and the thick gold chain around his neck.

'*Aaaaaaaaach...*' he sighs as he throws the document to me. 'What I am doing here? *Neeeeext...*'

I walk in haste down the long marble slippery corridors of the Athens Airport. At the exit, four customs officers drink coffee and smoke; they look annoyed by our presence. It's seven o'clock in the morning anyhow. With hand gestures, they shoo everyone out: I should have taken with me the forbidden flower seeds I was asked to bring.

Out in the fresh air; it is a warm, mild, intimate day; just flying in for three weeks.

'For you ... No meetings ... no distractions...'

I am anxious and curious, for mother and motherland. You are becoming sentimental again.

On the bus to Piraeus. Grim urban landscape, speech-less buildings, dirty streets: the sad spectacle of a city in meltdown. It seems as if the garbage collectors are permanently on strike.

Something is happening. Yes, it is: people move frantically up and down. I think that there must be an accident along the road – but no, it's the same again: some workers are protesting and they block the traffic.

Two hours of immobility. I want to make a phone call but I fall asleep in the bus.

Finally, I reach Mother's home – the ancient dwelling I abandoned so many decades ago. She stands at the door immense, small, primeval. (Her name is Anastasia but here she will be simply called Mother, capitalised, as she transcends all descriptions.)

'Why are you so late?' she asks.

Kisses, hugs and tears; more kisses, hugs and tears.

'Let me have a shower and some sleep; I will explain everything.'

'Always the same excuses...' she replies pensively.

Shower, change clothes, in bed. Massaging my swollen feet, trying to sleep as she watches the news and constantly shouts:

'You scumbags, filthy criminals, obscene crooks...'

She keeps talking endlessly to the television. Loneliness or helplessness?

But I fall asleep.

Later in the afternoon: the whole neighbourhood comes through the door. I want to keep my eyes closed – yet impossible. I get up and play the role of the repatriated emigrant. I have brought with me two lamb skins (*How soft ... Australian lambs must be so healthy and big...)*, four kangaroo skins (*They look like enormous rats...)*, a clock with the Harbour Bridge (*Beautifuuul...)*, two plastic Opera Houses (*It looks like the Parthenon...)* and several plastic koalas (*Can I have one for good luck?).* I know how to seduce my audience.

The discussion grows more serious:

'So far away ... Did you say twenty four hours by plane?'

'Yes, I did say twenty four hours by plane.'

'Well, you are here now, we will watch television together.'

I start dozing off, hovering between sleep and deterritorialisation, until a set of sentences is formed in my mind.

Greece, the old country: everything collapsed here in 2009 – and where we thought there was an affluent modern country, its social fabric disintegrated, its economy all but vanished, its political system imploded. I am to give reports about its free fall into disorder and nihilism. I am to watch the unravelling of the dominant civil order, the dissolution of its imaginary logotypes, the disintegration of its self-perception; detect absence where there was profusion, loss where there was exuberance, emptiness where there was excess.

I am listening now to her voice again:

'*You scumbags, filthy criminals, you obscene crooks...*'

On celestial Orphic hymns, Eurydice ... Bring me back from the shadows.

It's around seven o'clock when I open my eyes. It is only afternoon here; in the soft city of Sydney, it is already past midnight. The phone rings.

Eleni: 'Welcome ... Welcome ... Can we meet around midnight?'

Oh no, I must show the impact of my Protestant conversion.

'No, I can't. Nine thirty at the latest and by ten thirty I will be in bed.'

'Well, are you going to bed with the chickens?' She uses an impersonal proverb, which means she is annoyed.

'Yes I am.'

'Ok, then, let's meet on Monday at one, in Athens.'

'Where?'

'Let's meet first at Café Russo, on Aiolou Street and then we go to Syntagma Square, there is a new café close to the Parliament.'

On Monday. What's the day today? The Parliament? I have always felt guttural hatred towards the ugliest building in the country, the cathedral of all corruption, criminality and crude vulgarism. Yet all social life revolves around it: ugliness attracts lost souls.

The phone keeps ringing, sounds and noises scratch my ears as I am falling slowly in and out of sleep. Later, that night. I get up, like a somnambulist. Where am I? I walk out to the balcony and confront the dark city face to face. Classicist fantasies away, Athens looks like a science fiction city, dense, breathless and impenetrable. In the working class areas you can clearly see how people relate to space, constantly challenged by territorial imperatives. In the plutocratic areas it is the same feeling only in reverse: fewer buildings take up more space. Everywhere public areas shrink, open spaces disappear, the city devours. This makes people edgy, irascible, aggressive. A sense of disconnection prevails. Everything happens accidently, randomly, involuntarily. I feel like smoking – but stop there.

A thought: *'My duty, yes, my Kantian duty: the moral exploration of the city, the ethical mapping of its reality.'*

The church bells are tolling. The dawn service is greeting the rise of the solar god.

A second thought: *'Athens awaits a Charles Dickens to make visible its bewitching nostalgia for the formless and the unillumined'.*

I need coffee I will do anything for a cup of coffee. I must get out, I must walk the streets and take the snap shots that will weave a story out of the plotless unpredictability of everyday existence.

But first coffee, coffee please.

Day 2

Out I am, walking towards the centre of Piraeus, early mid-day. I notice: drab, shabby, cheap clothes. I remember more glamorous dress sense several years ago, especially around the 2004 Olympics. But, now, no style, no colour, no eccentricities: a throng of gray textile incongruities prevails. Around me: garbage everywhere (on strike), no transport (on strike too), a big rally of some workers on strike also at the centre of the city. Revolutionary songs (*The International)*, Leninist slogans (*Law is the right of the working class!)*, loud music (scratchy recordings from the seventies). Everything is bizarre, suggestive of other eras, unreal, in brief pathological.

The moment of illumination: As I am walking, trying to reconnect, somehow confused and drowsy, in the midst of hills of rubbish, suddenly the pale face of an elderly man pops up, out of a big garbage bin, raising two raw fish in both hands against the warm sun of the noon.

'Look, what I found...' he shouts. 'Look ... oh yes, yes, yes ... Food, food...' A prolonged manic laughter follows.

Soon, two other men appear and then a woman; they jump into the bin and yell in Greek and other languages:

'There is more! There is more! *Foooood* ... *foooood*...'

At least five more people arrive and scramble into the bin. More fish is found, tomatoes, vegetables and some morsels of rotten meat. Without fighting, they share everything, as if an innate form of pecking order exists between them, a code of survival based on mutual concessions. I am speechless. I feel lost. I am furious.

This event is my first encounter with the horror of the real; it sets the key for what follows.

The revolutionaries on the other side of the square look at them contemptuously.

'Look at the lumpenproletariat,' one says, shaking his head in anger and his hands in didactic severity. 'Come and join the struggle,' he shouts, raising his fist against invisible enemies. He carries on with his preaching:

'With their alienation, they undermine the revolutionary struggle, and delay the inevitable overthrow of neo-liberal capitalism.'

I know this automatised rhetoric. I think I know him who talks right now. Oh yes, yes, I can recognise his face above the three gold chains around his neck. What is his name? I used to call him 'Mr Everything to Everybody' for his surprising ability to change colours according to circumstances. Yes, I remember his name now. He remembers me too.

'*Hullooooo,* Australian,' he says. 'What are you doing here? I thought you were settled for good in the dollhouse of a country you chose to live in.'

That's real resentment and aggression from the very start. Anyhow he never liked me, which remains mutual.

'What happens in the motherland?' I ask somewhat ironically.

'The case is clear: foreigners want to buy our assets cheaply, own the islands, steal our oil deposits, take over our monuments, the Acropolis, the museums and even your birthplace, Olympia, for peanuts. We are under a new German occupation.'

Ah, yes, the conspiracies, against us, so many conspiracies.

We were friends, back then, in the late seventies. He started eloping from one party to the other as they changed in power. 'Change of government gives more options to the citizens who want to get involved!' He told me back in 1981. More options for him meant public positions, tax exemptions, bonuses, various invisible perks, paid travels and endless funding of shadowy projects without accountability – and if requested, an early retirement at fifty five, although you could still work as a senior without paying any taxes.

'But don't you feel embarrassed at all?' I ask. 'You studied law and you were appointed director of the committee for naval communications, then you moved to the committee for weapons and finally to the educational committee for digital technology, without being able to use a computer. Without any knowledge of English, to the Greek Press Office in London.'

'Never,' he replies with absolute certainty. 'I deserved every position because I served my party since I was fourteen years old.'

'So you became a director of some of the most critical industries not on the basis of your qualifications but because the party imposed you? Don't you have any sense of responsibility – I mean personal sense of responsibility?'

'No, I don't,' he replies obviously annoyed. 'Only the state has responsibility, not the individuals working for it. And we don't need specialists in our country. We need people who know how to manipulate the status quo.'

I am annoyed by his cynicism.

'This is the way you become the system – and supposedly you were fighting against it.'

'Well, you think so because you never took power, that's why.' (He turns nasty, now.)

'I suppose that it is correct', I say. 'Did I ever want to take power?' I ask. 'And you know very well that I had the opportunity.'

'It is only natural and necessary,' he replies, 'for us, the children of the underprivileged class, to desire the re-distribution of wealth. It's the only way to annihilate the enemies who persecuted us during the forties and fifties.'

I become impatient:

'The Greek Civil War has become the justification for every kind of self-serving ideology that has brought this country to sterility and disgrace. And always blaming foreigners, as if they took arms against other Greeks. Besides, you were born in the sixties,' I laugh. 'Is this what they call trans-generational trauma?'

'We want revenge for what happened then. And I am not alone. We are thousands, hundreds of thousands...' He shouts at me and moves his fists up and down.

'But your *"revenge"* has been translated into money and positions as you have been working *with* the people who supposedly persecuted your family in the past.'

'This does not mean that I agree with them.'

It is useless: camera obscura in action. I am talking about ethics and meritocracy, sounding so foolish and naive and outlandish, 'so Australian', as he says, 'silly Protestant moralisation...'

'It's all about us, the family, the party ... and social solidarity...' he grunts.

'And certainly not about any political project,' I retort.

Resentment in the atmosphere. I had enough of his negative aura. I become personal.

'How is your mother?' I ask but he doesn't reply. He turns his back and disappears in the crowd.

But more about him later: keep extrapolations to a minimum.

Later that Saturday. I am alone. I recall moments, episodes, incidents. Yet memories are never enough to guide you into the present. I start cleaning the library of dust. I find some forgotten letters from Canada. The phone rings, Panayiotis, an old friend from university days, invites me to a party.

'I don't do parties anymore and it is already eight.'

'Life begins now,' he replies.

'Well, it is when it ends for me.'

Stay in, reflect and wait. I cannot concentrate in this place, so much noise and phone ringing. There is no silence anywhere. You don't have a minute to take a step back and think. You are always on the run, faster and faster; you are exhausted and confused but here they call it excitement and euphoria.

Yet the unexpected always appears unconditionally.

Around eight thirty, two mythological creatures knock on the door. Mrs Felicity and her husband Nicko, simple, imposing, untouched by history, above all circumstances – chthonian. Two benevolent spirits who could endure anything and anyone, and who would stand firm at their place even during the eruption of a volcano.

I hadn't appreciated them before; they are odd, in a good way, but not so very odd as to have excited my intellectual superiority. They embody the untold stories of chthonian powers, the link between collective history and personal adventure.

Nicko never really knew his parents. They were killed, during a German bombardment in 1942. He became an orphan at five years old, survived the Germans, fought during the Civil War with the government, became a sailor in the early fifties, came back and reinvented himself as a master chef, then sailed away again, returned and started a restaurant, then a second restaurant, then lost all his money, started working for the national lotteries and retired in the year 2000 at seventy, although he regrets retirement: 'I have so much more to give!'

Mrs Felicity is his second wife; the first abandoned him, still pregnant, while he was sailing in India, in the early sixties.

'I never forgave her,' he says bitterly.

When he came back in 1959, by accident he became the master chef for the prime minister of the country.

'He was the most disgusting man I had ever met,' he declares contemptuously. 'I was serving him the best food every day and I witnessed some of his most confidential conversations with his ministers. I can't remember their names now, a short man, for example, and another one, really tall, with big ears. They were talking about the "multitude" and the "rabble" with hatred and disgust. I couldn't believe it! I had voted for them but after what I heard from his mouth I have always abstained from voting.'

He is agitated, somehow aloof, which is his own defence mechanism. Like a dandy however, impeccably dressed even so late, smoking endlessly slim Spanish cigarillos with exotic aromas:

'Only Spanish,' he points out emphatically looking with love at the white smoke. 'The French ones are not aromatic enough!'

'The hypocrisy of the whole thing,' he continues. 'I have been wondering for decades now: who were the nation of so many politicians, army generals, colonels and so many others who govern this country?'

He pauses and then: 'I had to resign after three years of working for him. I met so many people at his office, from all walks of life, humiliating themselves in front of his majesty, begging for favours, for positions, for money, for connections, for just about anything. It was really horrible. I grew up in poverty and insecurity. I never lost my dignity and self-esteem by stooping so low.'

Deep breath. 'One day he had some guest from an island; they were asking for the building of a hospital.

"You haven't voted for us," he yelled at them. "If you can change this in the next elections, it will happen!" "We will do so, by all possible means!" They promised. This is how public construction works were decided. They were both very happy. I had prepared the best food, lamb casserole with herbs and lemon – my specialty. I was happy with my work. But as I was serving it, he started shouting and yelling that his fork had some finger prints on its precious silver! I was shocked. "Mr President," I said. "I polished it myself, five minutes ago." He went mad, jumped up, threw a tantrum, spoke incomprehensibly and left the room.'

'That was really pathological,' I say. 'Real hubris.'

'I don't know your fancy word,' he replies. 'Nobody ever pays any attention to the existence of small people. We are tools, instruments, mere appendages to a machine operated by the great and the greater. Didn't he understand that even in my insignificance I had my own self respect?'

'No, I am afraid that there are some people who never understand.'

'I tendered my resignation, the next day, and left without compensation. I took the first ship to India and from there to Manila. Another four long years in distant seas. I never understood his behaviour, never! And never forgot that horrible foul language!'

'He changed, Mr Nicko, after 1974.'

'Because of de Gaulle: his ambition to be like him – I know.'

He is obviously informed.

'At least de Gaulle was proud to be French – unlike his copy.'

(Oh yes, *pour la France, pas pour les Français*...')

'I must tell you more stories about his entourage.'

I am in no mood for anecdotes.

'Tell me more about you, Mr Nicko,' I reply.

He looks more responsive yet distrustful.

'Why would you like to know about me?'

'I find you much more intriguing that those troublemaking non entities.'

He smiles. He looks content.

'I lived through so many things, so many words were said in front of me, in a way, they were about me; but who cares about servants?'

Mother is listening; Mrs Felicity understands that her husband must go first. As we are sitting around the table, lights, television and everything electric plunge into pitch black darkness: black-out again.

Are they on strike again or is the infrastructure disintegrating?

Lights go off all over the city. Darkness. Suddenly we immerse ourselves into silence. It is almost nine thirty. Silence. The four of us in the dark, scented smoke still in the air, the echo of his story around the room. We enter soundless immobility. It is as if we want simply to be there, in each other's presence. We don't move. We remain open. We remain. We gather, we are gathered, falling into the void that sustains human relations.

The lights come back with a resounding incandescence as power is restored. We feel sad, lost, somehow alienated.

Mr Nicko says: 'Well after this, let's talk again tomorrow.'

He opens the door and leaves in imperial slowness.

It is Saturday around midnight. As I try to sleep, I recall the first day I arrived in Australia almost twenty five years ago: the suggestive openness of Sydney, the luxury of recreating yourself, the desire to find a self whose symbolic existence is not reduced to its biological elements or its biographical particularities.

The bells again. Distant chanting, there must be a church somewhere close, oh yes, the Old Calendarist Church. And next to it, a Seventh Day Adventist Church. And just a few corners further, the clandestine mosque. All of them under the dominant shadow of huge Byzantine domes. Such embarrassing proliferation of religious theatres...

I must thank somebody for all these adventures but the years passed and we have grown old: we are always late in thanking anyone who has helped us.

It is around four o'clock in the morning – obviously I cannot sleep.

Day 3

Mother wants to go to church; a thing that I stopped doing for the fear of demonic possession. She insists:

'Hagia Sophia? The church of your childhood ... Don't you remember the pranks you played on the priest there? With the blessed bread and the holy communion?'

I remember that once I broke a tear gas capsule under the altar and father Eusthathios started crying ... Yet I remember no other prank about the blessed bread, unless I ate it before it was blessed ... For the sake of some ancient pranks I decide to go along.

We arrive; we look around, a crowd of faithful people, dressed in shining plumage, slowly walk up the stairs into the luminous cavities of the church. But it had to happen to us – of course. Before entering the courtyard at the gate two policemen block the entrance:

'Step aside,' they shout pushing back people violently. 'The Metropolitan is arriving!'

We stop and look. A stretched black limousine parks outside the gate. Twenty soldiers appear out of nowhere and stand still presenting arms along a red velvet carpet of unfathomable length. The metropolitan emerges like an enormous pelican, tall, slim and hydraulic, with his long beard, swaggering and strutting as he is struggling to balance the weight of three enormous gold crosses around his neck. His long right hand is swaying left right and centre an enormous pastoral staff made of silver or platinum – the shepherd of souls has arrived in sartorial magnificence and good taste.

He saunters pompously to the entrance of the church blessing the crowds who stand in utter silence and holy terror. Then he sweeps into the open mouth of his den. The bells are tolling uncontrollably. I think of the poor soldiers standing still. The enormous black limousine is groped by children. We are lost and confused under attack by kitsch, crassness and the legendary Christian humility.

'What was that?' I ask.

'Let's go away from here,' Mother says. 'This is not a place for people who believe.'

'This is so theological!' I whisper reverentially.

She shrugs her shoulders:

'Theological or non-theological, let's go for some delicious sweets around the corner...'

I lose the precious opportunity to relive my childhood pranks.

Not far away, towards the pastry shop, the miracle happens. Piraeus, the dirty, filthy, stinky city of industrial opportunism is transformed. It is music we hear. Authentic music. Not that deafening, pre-fabricated, con sumable bouzouki music, *bon pour l'Occident.* It is simple, mono-tonic, on few chords, yet rich in colour, tone and melody.

'Who plays this music? Where is it coming from?' I ask.

Mother replies:

'Oh, you have been away for so long. New people have moved in. It must be Mr Clearhos, the musician from Albania. Let's pay him a visit.'

She approaches the house and rings the bell.

'Mr. Clearhos,' she says looking through the window at the street level. 'This is my son from Australia who just heard your music and likes it.'

We are invited in. He is about sixty, gray hair, blue eyes, stooping, unshaven, with a cheeky smile on his face. Subdued but not conquered.

He arrived some twenty years ago. Alone, after having walked on foot over the huge mountains along the borders.

'Snow, everywhere,' he says. 'Mist, ice, wolves, soldiers shooting randomly, the mafia after you, for anything they could steal. But I kept this old instrument with me a gift of my grandfather before his was lost in 1972.'

On the walls, photographs of composers, Mozart, Brahms, Rimsky-Korsakov, Khachaturian, together with

Greek musicians, Vamvakaris, Tsitsanis and Theodorakis. Albanians also, Qazim Ademi and Fatime Sokoli (I think).

'Do you know anything about Albanian music?' he asks.

'Not really,' I reply. 'Except of course about the astonishing polyphonic folk songs.'

'It is strange,' he responds. 'Greeks know next to nothing about their neighbours, despite the fact that our histories are so connected.'

'This is for you,' he continues. 'So that you may remember your other life in this city.'

He starts playing the *instrument*: a soft mournful dirge comes to life, made of smooth and soothing sounds, separate from each other, leaving space for silence to be felt as sonic presence, accompanied by deep breaths, evolving into sighs and gradually to wild groans, *ich, ach, oi, oi.* Then, the three chords of the long necked instrument start being frantically plunked, new vibrational densities emerge, sounds of anger, fury, despair – jumping out of the Dionysian ecstasy of nothingness. Suddenly, he stops playing, he sighs deeply and starts crying – all Balkan music ends in crying. His music lasts for less than a minute. It is his catharsis, and our exposure to the re deeming transfiguration of cosmic sonorities. I feel physically exhausted.

'That's sublime,' I say, me who never liked folk tunes.

'It's from my heart,' he replies. 'I suffer, I am in pain. I left behind my history, my home, the rose-garden I planted. This music is what remains of them: fragments of forgotten tunes, moments of happiness amidst days of incomprehensibility. Now, who am I? I cannot sing any more because I live only with memories ... Not with emotions ... Only memories and nostalgia; and you cannot make good music by recollecting what is lost. You must be burning with the intensity of the present!'

Mother intervenes:

'You are very much loved and respected, Mr Clearhe, very few people achieve this...'

I stop her because the last part would have been 'very few people from Albania.'

'Why don't you record your music?' I ask.

'Nobody is interested in this old style,' he says in resignation. 'After the fourth chord was added to the bouzouki, the *instrument* became good only for exhibitionistic virtuosity. It lost its authentic sound which created a continuum from Corsica to India. The addition opened a chasm which was filled with vulgar dancing, sound amplifiers and inane lyrics – and I am telling you: songs must never have lyrics, only sighs and cries.'

He stops and tells me didactically, as he points at me with his finger:

'Beware of the virtuosos! Under their dexterity, they always hide their lack of feeling. Good music is like the human voice – it breaks and crumbles: its pitch changes and rhythm becomes lame. Like the voice of Maria Callas ... Only through its ups and downs you can understand that there is an active mind guiding the hands that hold the instrument.'

Suddenly two gentlemen open the door. 'My friends,' he introduces to us: 'Muhtar and Elian. We will be going together down to the open market busking for money. I must pay the rent too.'

Muhtar has his accordion with him. In broken Greek he says:

'Made in Germany, back in 1912. It is still *megaaaaalo!*'

Elian from Kosovo with a peculiar clarinet.

'Turkish clarinet,' he says. 'Made in Istanbul, 1916 – *maaaaagnificent* sound...'

'We must go now,' Mr Clearhos says. 'Thank you for coming in. Next time I will play you music by a strange character, Gurdjieff, if you know him...'

What! What did he just say? Did he say Gurdjieff? Did he? But he goes to the other room. Before leaving, Mother follows him and discreetly slips fifty euros in his jacket. I rush out in anger – she destroys my Gurdjieff moment.

'What did you do?' I ask in fury.

'Well, Mr. Australian, you do have money always in your pockets but he doesn't. He is unemployed and needs food. But then all artists must be hungry in order to produce good art – don't you think?'

What should I say to this? She has a point, indeed more than one and that's confusing. She knows how to make me angry, too.

It is already noon and I feel the disorientating dizziness of jetlag. Home. I need sleep.

The same night; I cannot sleep. I must listen to the voice of the ordinary people who have no place of consolation to go: *this is not a place for people who believe...*

Don't waste time. Focus on the specificity of the common. Do not lose sight of what is habitually covered by generalisations, idealised abstractions and grand narratives. Under the crust of theories, the concreteness of fundamental presences.

Let us now praise famous men...

Day 4

Time for Athens. A pilgrimage, a duty, an adventure. I get up around seven. The fragrant instant coffee gives the tune for the compromises I have to endure. Morning talk:

'I am going to Athens.'

'What time will you be back?'

'Sometime in the evening.'

'There is a good Turkish movie on. Don't miss it.'

'Don't worry – I will miss it.' But I won't.

I walk to the station; through old factories, dirty streets and angry people. Nobody ignores any opportunity to humiliate the other. Gone are the days when strangers talked to you, instinctively following the formulas of civilised distance. Now they just rush and keep talking about money; if they could, they would pass though you.

Meanwhile they are all on strike. The trains work until eleven; then on strike too, until four. At the entrance, an old man holds a plastic bottle and pours water on his head. He is screaming: 'Mother of god, Mother of god ... Give me a sign...' and pours more water on his body. He is staring at the sky. 'Where is the sign? Where is the sign?' His voice is full of sadness. The sky remains silent. Around him, other homeless people lying on the footpath, smoking and looking at him patiently, like reclining Etruscans.

The train is almost empty. But soon six men come in. They look wild as they roam up and down the carriages. And yes, inevitable, they all sit next to me.

'Hi! Hi! Do you have a cigarette!'

'No.'

'Why not? We want cigarettes.'

'I do not smoke. And we are not allowed to smoke in here.'

They all start laughing. Laughing, laughing, louder and louder. The train reaches Faliron. Why do I attract ambiguities? Nobody comes in. We move on as they start talking about doctors, nurses and tablets.

'Do you have any tablets with you?' They ask winking with meaning.

'I've got only aspirins,' I reply.

'Aspirins ... ha, ha, ha ... He is got aspirins, ha ... ha ... ha...'

One of them comes close to my face.

'Guys,' I smile. 'Do you want me to move to another seat?'

'Ha ... ha ... ha ... No, no brother ... Do not get upset ... We just got out of Dafni.'

'Oh, the mental hospital, I am sorry, I couldn't possibly know.'

'The loony bin ... *Yeaaaa,* we are all the children of the nuthouse. *Yeaaaa,* of the nuthouse...'

We reach the next station. Four youngsters come in. They understand the situation and don't miss the opportunity to start making fun.

'Hi, wackos ... kookies ... loonies ... Did you take your medication today, you nutters?'

The six men abandon me, and move towards them. I am left alone to breathe. We are at the next station. Three beggars enter, as the fight goes on. They want to sing and they sing. Each one with his own tune. Pandemonium. Next station. Hundreds of people come in. The abolition of distance between us, of the territorial imperative, imposes a feeling of distress and discomfort, as our private space has been invaded. We get edgy, irate, jaded. I close my eyes. I am trying to remember a poem, the beginning of Milton's *Paradise Lost,* but only Auden springs to mind:

> *The desires of the heart are as crooked as corkscrews.*
> *Not to be born is the best for man*
> *The second best is a formal order...*

Omonoia at last. I rush out, longing for the missing formal order. The madmen and the non-madmen keep fighting behind.

Deep breath. I go up the stairs; Omonoia Square, the centre of Athens. The grand spectacle of a public space for everyone. I remember it well. It hasn't changed but the clear weather makes it so transparent that you think you are in a small village. Café Neon, with its enormous Venetian mirrors, its aromatic coffee and its sexual tension is closed. Half of the former glorious shops are closed. The left side looks like a deserted village. On the other side, towards Athinas Street life at its busiest still goes on. There, you can detect strange presences; men shaking little plastic sachets in both their hands exhibiting them in public. Drugs. In plain daylight. And it looks like cocaine to me: 'the little sugar,' as they call it. The police look and laugh. I step into the old café and order its famous yogurt with honey. It is still early in the morning. The city is not up yet. People stare at you while pretending to read the morning papers.

An elderly gentleman asks in broken English:

'Where are you from? You look foreigner...'

I want to respond in Greek, but why?

'From Canada,' I reply. Yes, why should I tell him the truth? Anyhow, I do the same with all cabdrivers in Sydney.

'Oh, Canada', he exclaims. 'Toronto, Montreal, and ... and ... What's the name of the capital city?'

'Canberra,' I reply.

'Oh, yes, Canberra,' he consents and turns to the newspaper again.

Meanwhile, as time is suspended, I am transported back to nineteen seventy six, when at the very same spot I saw Jean Paul Sartre walking, small and almost blind, holding hands with a beautiful woman: death and the maiden. This is a place for meeting remarkable and unremarkable people.

In the corner towards the Town Hall, I see the terrified eyes of a northern European girl. She notices. With broken Greek she says:

'I am hungry.'

'I won't give you any money,' I say. 'I will buy you food.'

'Okay, buy me food.'

I buy for her anything I can find, together with milk and coffee. She squats on the footpath. She starts eating and drinking everything.

'I am sorry,' I explain. 'I thought that you wanted money for drugs.'

She laughs, as milk is split all over her beautiful face.

'Don't worry,' she mocks me. 'I have my blond pussy for that kind of money. All Greek men want to be sucked and pay lots of money...!'

Eleni, meeting at one. Café Russo. The old part of Athens, Aiolou Street, now a place for intellectuals, journalists and artists – or for all those who fake it. I try to overhear: *'The previous prime minister suffered a nervous breakdown; he is in Switzerland recovering in the Alps.' 'The former prime minister is travelling the world giving lectures about solving the crisis – the person who created the crisis. He never visited his electorate.' 'The minister for finance is gone to Holland; he has big business there and he will never come back.' 'It was discovered that the previous minister of defence (the one who almost became the prime minister) received bribes from Germany to buy a number of submarines, totally useless to the defence of the country – and dangerously tilting.'*

I have had enough. Nothing else to talk about besides the corruption of politicians.

Eleni arrives. 'Let's get out of here,' I say. 'Please, I had enough of the same stuff for so many decades.'

'What happened to the days,' I ask her, 'when we all talked about new books, ideas, movies and distant places to visit? What happened to the days when we talked about our dreams?'

Eleni: 'All gone, gone forever. A culture of cynicism has been established. I am telling you: during the last five years I saw an unconditional regress, a relapse to conscience-less tribalism.'

'It is so obvious – and yet nobody wants to admit it. They all talk about corruption and conspiracies but the most obvious reality is the breakdown of civility.'

'Some of us reacted already before the Olympics of 2004. Others saw it as a negative symptom of change. You might remember the notorious statement: *there is no development without corruption.* But it was a systematic strategy of the political order to neutralise its citizens – and now it backfired and turned against them.'

'It is sad to realise that the main enemy of your society is its own political administration.'

'Well, that's the case with our country. For almost thirty years people took office determined not to do anything but simply enjoy its privileges – and distribute them to their clients. They brought Greece into the club of sharks, the European Union, and thought that the only role it could play was that of the Red Riding Hood – dancing through the dark forest of aggressive capitalism with Mediterranean euphoria and *joie de vivre.*' She adds:

'I think that it was a deliberate ideological policy to keep the population under constant infantilization. By flattering its primal narcissism and constructing a sinister anti-world of self-serving Europeans, they imposed the amoral certainty of a presumed cultural exceptionalism, legitimised by the appeal of the classics and consecrated by the rituals of the clergy.'

'And the Left? Didn't they get it? Any hope?'

'The Left parties all children of the same authoritarianism; and as such they suffer from messianic escapism. Indeed their constant attack against 'neo-liberal capitalism' indicates their naive belief in a Pol-Potian agrarian society. They want to replace all industry with farming, olive oil production, wine, honey combing and raisin exports. To substitute digital technology and computers for a healthy Mediterranean diet! They are such traditionalists that they cannot even understand in Marxist terms what world-views such agrarian communities institute.'

'But is their confusion only ideological?'

'Because they are products of an autocratic society and have been formed by totalitarian ideas, they chose to ignore the horizontal small dialogues within their society. They are interested only in metaphysical speculations and platonic abstractions, like capitalism, socialism, social revolution and the usual – everyday reality does not exist for them as for every Platonist.'

'I lost all confidence in them,' I say, 'when in the last elections, I heard their leader declaring *"With us in power, the people will govern".* I couldn't believe the frightening prospect of another populist regime: Mussolini plus Peron plus Papandreou. A new brand of political ideology prevails, the only political ideology produced in this country: *ethnopopulism,* or even more *ethnotribalism,* a mixture of tribal nationalism and pre-modern communitarianism. In the era of postmodernism, that's the best recipe for another disaster – and I am talking about a disaster in self-perception, since the country must be addicted to political and economic catastrophes. Don't they know what comes out of a snake's egg?'

'Well,' she replies. 'They fantasise that they maintain their integrity and innocence while being involved in Machiavellian power games. The absence of moral considerations makes them nothing but instruments for revenge and not agents for justice or change. In the end nobody believes them either – but they vote for them out of despair, resentment or self-interest.'

'I don't know of many politicians with moral considerations,' I say.

'I don't know many either,' she agrees. 'But it is their moral conformism that makes them so ineffectual: the disentanglement of the moral from the political. We all know that they are not telling the truth – but we are all equally satisfied with lies.'

I am about to ask something but voices and commotion intervene. As we walk up a back street towards Syntagma, hundreds of people are gathered around a small square. A man from a big truck throws plastic bags with vegetables at them. People are fighting to catch them as invisible hands fling them out from within the vehicle. They punch each other, some fall to the ground, screaming, shouting, swearing. This is gritty cinematic hyper-realism. Yet everything looks choreographed and staged: the cameras are lurking close by.

Eleni: 'The worst consequence of this crisis is that we have all lost our dignity and self-respect. Even those who pretend to remain calm and in control, and they are very few.'

I reflect: the incident illustrates the de-civilising process that has conquered both public and personal life in the country.

Yet Eleni talks about the energy and the tension of the city, which, as I feel it, is only rage and disorder.

'Eleni,' I beg. 'Let's go somewhere quiet.'

'Now what?' she scoffs me. 'Reality has become so hard to swallow? Probably this is what we always have been. Disguised predators, scared animals who never managed to transform their darkness into lucid self-reflection.' She stops melancholically.

'Suspend your expectations when you visit a country shaken by such crisis. You are not here to recognise yourself but to look at the life of others which has nothing to do with you.'

Before arriving in Syntagma, we see on television that an anarchist group of hormonally agitated youths had planted a bomb at a shopping mall. The explosion didn't happen. People got out in time and the police found the bomb. The anarchist group later sends out their proclamation: *'Total rejection of civilisation for total liberation. We hit the shopping mall because it is a gigantic graveyard of human beings and true values.'*

Oh, *'true values'*, nineteen years old moralists who know everything about true values! When they are later arrested, at an attempted heist of a country bank, it is revealed that they are all children of super-wealthy families, never having worked for a single day in their lives, with visceral hatred of the bourgeois society of their parents – against the Father yet unable to commit parricide. They use slogans from Malatesta and Bakunin, and declare that: *'Our political choice was not to be present when institutions call them.'*

One of them must have read Louis Althusser ... Yes, the famous epistemological break... We are all *interpellated ...* and all the other bullshit that French intellectuals have concocted in order to substitute the rhetoric of their self-dramatisation and despair for the political experience of a collectivity.

'Eleni,' I say, 'this is so farcical! Twenty year old kids confident that they know the only true values of social life? This is more narcissism than politics! The Nietzschean bonfire of vanities and self indulgence...'

'I know, but they are traumatised, poor kids ... They live without hope.'

'I don't know of many people, who haven't been traumatised. But these kids mess around with the lives of other innocent people. From what I read, they killed an accidental bystander, they possessed massive weapons and robbed two banks in order to fund their revolutionary struggle against the system. This is ridiculous ... Do other people have the right to exist and not find themselves entangled in the private nightmares of the intellectual aristocracy? Why do others have to pay for the panic of a privileged minority?'

'You have become a Protestant moralist,' she says sarcastically.

'Yes, I have. Because the chaos of living can be understood only if you shape it around ethical considerations. The rest is only masked moral solipsism.'

'We are in a state of what the Italians call *"low intensity civil war"* ,' she says. 'We must fight back. Yet, I am very ambivalent myself about all these.'

'What about consent?' I ask. 'Why don't we understand that the true enemy is the forms of action we have adopted and by now we are unwilling to change or criticise, because we have become dependent on them?'

'That will be the end of our social history,' she tells me. 'Without conflict, without enemies, external or domestic, we cannot have an identity in this country. Our identity is articulated on what we do not want to be and not on what we are.'

Carl Schmitt again, I know, the enemy, the enemy that justifies what I am – the cleverest policy of the Greek power elites to impose artificial social bonds without national consciousness.

'Yet', I continue, 'you all seem deeply fascinated by such pretty and privileged rebels – ignoring what they are doing: by explaining their motives you think that you justify their actions.'

'We are drawn to the spell and the charm of such young fighters. Probably because we live in the confusion of perpetual adolescence, and we don't want to confront adulthood. You see,' she adds, 'you have lived most of your life in the Anglosphere, where childhood is revered and adolescence does not really exist. Here we have the opposite reality: childhood is immediately forgotten and we live till the end of time with the flurry and the fluster of our sixteenth year – and in all our life we struggle to immobilise time at that age or recreate its turmoil until we die.'

'I will write down this anthropological observation,' I say. 'But, yes indeed, it is sad. Especially when you see people in their sixties talking about revolution and rebellion from within the comforts of their bourgeois luxuries.'

As we talk, people in a café start fighting about the young rebels. One of them starts screaming: '*We will kill you all...*' He is in an epileptic rage ... '*Blood will cleanse this city...*' he shouts, '*Blood ... only blood...*' He sits down and takes a sip from his cappuccino. Another one, as he watches television, shouts: '*We must punish the Europeans by not allowing them to use any Greek words...*'

'Eleni, look at them ... Have I lost my mind? This is like a state of perpetual delusion which never allows for the individual drama to be told.'

She nods in near despair.

'There is no other way,' she says shaking her head. 'Only the way of collapse and catastrophe.'

It will start raining soon.

As we talk, a huge limousine carrying the most ruthless politician in the country passes by. I nostalgically recreate the moment when the conservative prime minister of Australia came into a pub, asked for a beer and started talking with us, who didn't vote for him, about cricket.

'I know nothing about cricket,' I said.

'Don't worry,' he replied, 'I know nothing about history either.'

I loved that dry sense of humour, the self-irony indicating the need for common spaces – but I never voted for his party.

A thought. I never liked Robert Frost; but his verse about the westward country '*Vaguely realising ... but still unstoried, artless, unenhanced...*' gives the key to understand the adventure of the individual in this country. Indeed, unstoried, artless, unenhanced. Alone, unreflective, plotless. I read: Marcel Proust has shown that lovers search for unhappiness. Athens always lets you down. So, I want to go home, to Australia. I want to hear about real problems: how crunchy Arnott's biscuits should be, why electricity prices went up by twenty cents, why a politician used three hundred dollars from his union credit card to visit a brothel, why the prime minister is not married, why sharks have come so close to the beaches. These are real problems, because they leave room for the epic tales of ordinary individuals to be heard, be storied and be articulated.

'Good bye, Eleni,' I say. 'I am really distressed. I shouldn't have come.'

She holds my hand and says:

'We must transubstantiate chaos into a tragic story, since we cannot make fun of ourselves. Yes, probably comedy would have had a deeper cathartic effect ... I wish I were Aristophanes – he was the only Greek who could tell true parables about human folly and stupidity.'

Day 5

Local supermarket. Two young girls outside:

'Milk, sir ... We want some milk!'

I enter, buy two litres for each one, give the bottles to them. They drink it immediately; as the milk is dripping from their mouths the youngest says:

'Any money, any money?'

I give them two euros each.

'Gypsies,' Mother says disparagingly. 'Always asking for money ... They will follow you now everywhere...'

They did: 'imprinting' is called. They follow those who show them kindness.

Mother insists: 'Do not encourage them! You don't know where they are coming from!'

'Mother', I say, 'I am an immigrant too...'

'But you are not gypsy ... And you have a job!' she replies triumphantly.

The two little girls understand. They return to the entrance of the supermarket waiting for the next imprinting to occur.

But there is no lazy day here. Trying to sort out some taxation issues which devastate my entire budget as

I am penalised for not having closed a receipt book which was used twice for three hundred drachmas, thirty five years earlier. Then struggling to make sense of the new taxation system according to which tax officers, irrespective of what you declare, make their own evaluation of your income. You must prove your innocence and that you don't make as much money as they think. I must visit the tax office.

'Take some cash with you to grease their palms,' Mother says. 'This is the only language they understand.'

I arrive at the tax office around nine in the morning; at least fifty people are waiting. 'Take a number from the machine,' the security man says. I take one, number 76, but no one follows them. Every time that somebody finishes, whispering with the tax officer, they all jump up and rush towards the counter. A mild melee follows, and all settle down again for several minutes. They all whisper with the officer – I wonder why...

I read Freud's *Interpretation of Dreams,* but after two hours of waiting not even this is not enough to make me forget time. I give up. I will come back tomorrow.

Out in the streets: huge piles of garbage everywhere, flies, stench, mosquitoes. Next to the piles, elegant and well designed shops. I take a walk down the main street of Piraeus along the harbor. I try not to remember, but everything comes back in an avalanche. The harbour, the city, the buildings, the clubs, the shops, the kiosks, the ferries, the sailors, the prostitutes, the pimps, the police men, the cinemas, the churches. Old days full of energy and anonymity, full of hope and perseverance; now everything stands as lack and loss and absence. The collapse made us a fatherless generation, deprived of the inscapes of our childhood. Everything is now a negative antitype of itself. What you see is a vacant space in the form of a building – prey to the poetry of departed deities.

Around most of the abandoned buildings, homeless, poor and illegal aliens are settled. They look at you with despair, envy, hatred. As I walk down their way, the police arrive. They encircle the area. They start shouting: '*Get up, get up, time to go home*...' laughing with sarcasm. They drag them out of their blankets, their paper boxes and rags, pushing them towards two police trucks. Some locals applaud, others remain silent. In fifteen minutes the place behind the empty tower, is cleansed of people but still full with rubbish. They all know that nobody will ever come to clean the area and collect the blankets and the teapots – the symbols of an ephemeral presence at this space.

Time to go back home – or anywhere.

Around seven Mrs Felicity arrives. She looks at me anxiously. My story, she silently implores, can I tell you my story? But the Turkish melodramas begin and we are forced into silence.

In between the story and the commercial breaks, we try to compile a narrative.

'I was born just before the war. My parents died during the terrible famine in forty-two. No help, no food, no home: only the church and later the UNRA helped me survive. Then the other war came, with the communists. Too many orphans, we had to be scattered around the country.'

She turns her attention to television.

'What is happening?' she asks.

'They are going to kill Silà,' Mother replies in horror.

'What is happening in Turkey even today, even today! What sort of minds do these people have?'

She turns to me. 'Where was I?'

'You were sent to the countryside.'

'Not far away. To the island of Salamis, but there was no school or anything else there. I grew up working in the fields; our payment was potatoes and fruit, occasionally milk.'

She turns to Mother: 'Did they kill her?'

'No, not yet. But look! They interrupt it for commercials. We cannot enjoy the story anymore.'

Again to me:

'I was thrown out of school and put into an institution for children with special needs. I grew up with torture, punishments and caning. Why did they treat children like that? I was only fourteen. The year after, I escaped. I had some relatives in the Peloponnese; and stayed with them for six years.'

She turns to Mother.

'It starts again. Poor Silà, she suffers because she is born in a backward region. Yet, she is dressed very well – very *chic*...'

They are watching Silà being abducted by two men. She is left alone in a deserted old house. A woman appears with a gun. *'Where is my baby?'* Silà shouts. *'This baby should have been mine,'* the other woman says. *'I gave birth to it,'* Silà screams. *'Yes, but it should have been mine*...' Silà howls: *'But it is mine*...' The gun points at her, camera close-up on the baby and then on the gun. Anxious music. A shot is heard. End titles. They are obviously both shaken.

'They stop it always at the most crucial moment! It is annoying! Tomorrow again!' Mother says.

'You must complete your story, Mrs Felicity.'

'Well, in the fifties things were not very good. For some reason, my relatives were labelled communists, so they were under constant supervision by the police. My uncle was exiled to one of the islands for over three years. Only women were at home. But the countryside around Corinth was so beautiful. Endless lemon and orange groves, olive trees, vineyards, and pine trees almost touching upon the sea. In springtime the fragrances of the budding trees made us hallucinate. We were losing our mind, you know, it was as if something strange was covering us and we couldn't escape it. Our little hut was close to the sea and one summer night I went out and in front of me dolphins were jumping in and out of the sea under the gigantic moon of August.'

'What happened next?'

'After so much happiness I couldn't stay there anymore. I decided to come to Piraeus. I couldn't find work. A lonely woman was always an easy prey. I changed ten jobs in one year. Finally, I worked as a cleaner in a hospital, then in some offices, then I worked in a factory, then in the railways, then in cruising ships around the islands. I cannot tell you what I have gone through – worse than what we see in Silà's story.'

She is upset.

'In April '67, Sunday, the twenty third, I got married my first husband. Something had happened then with the government, and we were not allowed to celebrate as we should. That was not a wedding – it was like the underground secret school – no dances, no songs, no nothing. Politicians never think about the life of other people...'

'It was a serious event, Mrs Felicity. The 1967 Dictatorship...'

'Yes, but we must live as well, you know. Anyhow,' she continues. 'After having started so badly, the marriage didn't last. Three years later, he was gone, leaving me alone with a child. I never saw him again.'

'Didn't he ever look for his child?'

'No, never. As I say to your Mother, never trust a creature with dangling bits between its legs.'

'That's so true...' Mother consents.

'Well, four years later I met Nicko accidently. We went to his restaurant. He looked at me, I looked back. That was it. I moved in. We decided to get married in November 1973, the twenty fifth, I think Sunday.'

I start laughing.

'You have the instinct for political upheavals...'

'Well, something with the students in the Polytechnic School now and my second wedding was also like the underground secret school. Politics destroyed my wedding for the second time...'

'But this marriage lasted...'

'He is a good man, Nicko,' she says. 'He knows how to get dressed. He was drinking heavily in the early eighties when he lost all his money. He came out of it. He is happy, despite the three cancers that torment him for the last fifteen years...'

'Cancer?'

'The doctors expected him to die ten years ago. He came home, started smoking, eating, dancing, going out – let's enjoy our last days – let's live as if there is no tomorrow – but he survived, he is seventy eight and he is pretty good.'

'What about your child?' I ask.

'Hush now,' she replies. 'The new Turkish show begins, *Tears of Love,* and its story is taken from my life.'

'Mrs Felicity...' I say but I am not allowed to finish my sentence...

'Hush, hush, hush,' she says ... 'The song in the beginning is very catchy; we love singing it with your mother.'

They both start crooning a Turkish song without knowing a word of the language.

It is only nine thirty at night; time for their common performance.

I am going to bed – but who can sleep when such angelic arias are heard?

Day 6

Tax office again: eight thirty in the morning. The officer, a woman with at least twenty rings around her fingers, and dyed carroty hair, is adamant:

'You must prove that your mother, who, as you have admitted, lives in the apartment which is under your name, does not pay you any rent – which in this case would have been taxable income, plus penalty for not having declared it.'

'Madam,' I protest, 'do you know many Greek sons who ask rent from their mother? Which planet are you from?'

'That's the law, sir.'

'Well it's up to you to prove that I receive money not to me that I am innocent.'

She forges on: 'I will make an estimate of three thousand euros per year for which nine hundred is your tax.'

Her dismissive tone infuriates me. I explode:

'I am not going to give you any money! I will take you to court! Where is the manager?'

I am furious, my voice is heard three storeys below. Security appears.

Just then, she gently adds: 'Let's negotiate the amount.'

That's it! 'Madam,' I scream, 'you are not going to receive a single euro from me! I am Australian and in my country we call people like you frauds and crooks...'

What did I just say? I am Australian? Finally I give identity to myself...

And in anger I walk out...

'My solicitor will contact you,' I shout.

Before leaving, I can hear the voice of the softly speaking woman:

'Fucking foreigners, they come here to tell us how to do our job...'

I had to quench my fury in two sweet pies and one cappuccino. The sun also rises and also sets. My fury is inflamed again when I receive the bill:

'Fifteen euros for two pies and one coffee?' I scream. But I submit.

Meanwhile, I am ready for my descent to the underbelly. I will visit the working class areas in the western suburbs. Egaleo, Dafni, Haidari and the city of Elefsis. Everywhere by bus: expose yourself to the landscapes of misery, observe the obscure trivialities of mundane freedom, locate signs of ethical resistance. As others visit museums, archaeological sites, art galleries, exhibitions and tourist attractions, I have the morbid pleasure of exploring first the working class areas in the cities I visit.

Thus starts our uneventful adventure in the western suburbs of Athens. A bus takes us to the central Egaleo square. In the past, it was a place of intense political activity. Later, when many cafés opened, lazy unemployed politicians took over – the era of Beelzebub, the eighties. In the following period, restaurants with cheap or not so cheap food. Now half of them are closed. The cafés are still full, with unemployed youngsters and slothful public servants. We move amongst them. Noisy traffic, dirty streets, huge bins in every corner full of all sort of refuse. Some of them are used for people to sleep in. We wanted to take photographs – but we resisted the pornography of suffering.

We see two crowds on both sides of the main streets: tax office on the left. Hundreds of people waiting to get in. They are yelling and screaming: the usual story – one clerk to deal with all. It is still morning, but the other five who supposedly should have been working are having their coffee break. On the other side, the bank: at least fifty elderly people, waiting for their pension to be paid. Aged and stooping people, some of them holding staffs, wait for their money. Every now and then, the bank door opens and some of them are allowed to come in, as others have finished and are coming out. At the moment we are going away, an old lady faints. As the security people bring her in, at least ten from those waiting sneak in – and the struggle begins. Somebody from the inside slams the door – an old man is hit on the nose and bleeds. We must go. Shouts and screams again.

We walk aimlessly: garbage everywhere, beggars, uneasiness. We see something strange: a bird is tied by a small rope around the branches of a lonely standing eucalyptus. Almost tears in my eyes, eucalyptus ... bush ... Australia, oh the fragrance of gumtrees, so far away from the bush. A dark man, probably from the subcontinent, asks for help, and all together, indigenous or non indigenous, bring two staircases together, hold them tight as the man climbs up the steps. With effort he reaches the branch and struggles for about five minutes to free the bird. The bird flies away. He comes down, people applaud, shake hands with him, a local woman kisses him:

'Well done, brave lad,' she says, 'May your mother be proud of you!'

They go back to their work.

We move on. Dafni. That's the real thing, indeed hyperrealism in action. On one side of the road the mental hospital. On the opposite side of the road, the medieval monastery. Quite symbolic, methinks. Recollection: twelve years old. With the school we are outside the monastery, attending the famous Dionysus wine festival. People drinking, singing and dancing. Late September, an unshaven man wearing a heavy winter coat comes close and says: 'Any cigarettes' No, we don't smoke, we are only twelve. He starts jumping up and down, happy and euphoric. 'No cigarette today, no cigarette, only medication, only tablets...' The school teacher: 'I have told you not to talk with mad people. Madness is contagious and who knows which one of you will follow him down that path ... You will end up in that huge building...' He points at the hospital, grey, drab and rectangular box of cement. We don't want to end up in there; so we rush into the monastery. We try to control our panic by surrendering to the polychromatic brilliance of Byzantine mosaics – we turn to religion out of the fear of madness. End of recollection.

Now: we are entering the monastery; restoration work still continues, since the 1997 earthquake. The frightful Jesus with the distorted hands on the dome; the elegant John and the tragic mother of god on the left side. Jesus' fingers have given me many nightmares as I child, ready as they are to pierce your eye with their distorted sharp nails. As we look around, we notice a young man, of dark complexion.

He talks: 'I am Muslim. But this is a truly sacred place.'

Broken Greek, he stands in the dark side of the church, wearing a long heavy coat, and military boots: he seems immersed into the atmosphere. We talk.

'Iraq,' he says. 'My parents were killed by Saddam. I was only two. Ever since I have been trying to find a home, Egypt, Syria, Lebanon, Saudi Arabia and unexpectedly, smuggled in with a cargo ship, this country, this place, this building. The nuns give me food, and let me sleep in an empty room. I will learn better Greek to talk *with* the paintings. We don't have paintings in my religions but these made me stop and think.'

He begins a weird asthmatic song, haunting and mournful.

'They call them mosaics,' I reply.

'I loved this place from the very first minute,' he says ignoring my point. 'I will stay here for some time.' We shake hands. Farewell.

A thought: a Sufi trapped in the garden of Satan.

Where are we now? Elefsis! How did we get here? We should have stopped at Haidari. But we didn't. What happened? Too much emotion, probably. Elefsis, the industrial paradise, the ancient refuge. The city busy and buzzy, yet an eerie emptiness covering the streets. People are moving in a frenzied manner, up and down, entering shops, groceries, cafés, offices. There are many stray dogs everywhere and countless cats; they look at each other with exhaustion, boredom, *l'ennuiè,* of the created life caused by other created life.

Look: a homeless man in the central square fills a small bowl with milk. Look: cats are approaching and start licking it. Look: from the butcher's shop, a young boy in white bloodstained apron throws out bones, meat cuts, and fat to the dogs. Look: they snatch them and go away. Flies everywhere.

Cars, trucks and a train pass by, leaving dust, disorder and fumes in the air. Two buses collide; two trucks block the entrance to one of the main streets. The face of an elderly woman looking down from her loft.

Motor bikes, the big smoke from the oil refineries, the endless flow of students exiting the school. The symphony of an industrial paradise. The stage reminds me of Dziga Vertov's eye-camera.

The ancient ruins surrounded by factories, shipyards and steel structures. Cats, dogs and birds scavenging through them. We want to enter but look, no – they are on strike. Anyhow, we didn't come here for these things. Cafeteria, *La Strada.* Sipping coffee, good coffee at last; around us the landscape of a sunken city.

Eerie silence again: it is as if sounds and voices come from a long distance. Where are we? Living moments: a priest in the emblematic black robes walks in front of us holding an umbrella. An elderly lady leaves a plastic bag next to a garbage bin. Hundreds of sparrows are flying everywhere in majestic shapes, hundreds, thousands maybe. They all try to find a space to sit on: but only the cafés exist – sitting there and drinking coffee is the actual manifestation of social despair and malaise.

Proustian moment: teaching at a local school, so many years ago, as we study Plato, students are upset, because it is November and six in the evening, dark and cold, and they want to go home, the last bus is around six fifteen, they live up in the mountains, in Mandra, they don't want to learn anything about Plato, they want to go home, it is cold, it starts raining, tonight some of them, must milk their goats and feed their livestock, alone in the wetness of the night, the mist of high altitudes, and the school asks them to do homework on maths, physics, geometry, Ancient Greek, English, Greek literature, psychology, philosophy, biology, and more, while they need sleep and rest, it takes them one hour by bus, it will be already seven thirty when they reach home, Plato does not help, maths do not help, biology does not help. 'Please, sir, let us go, we will miss the last bus and we don't know where to spend the night...' They all have permission to go. The teacher stays alone in the class, drowning himself in the oceanic pages of the *Symposium*. End of recollection.

We return defeated and demoralised, we always do. No archaeological sites, no museums, no Ithaca, not even our old school is there anymore. It has become a detention centre for illegal refugees. It is a distressing, frightening day. We are in the belly of the beast – this is what we want to see. Present patterns of living, the sense of felt time, the voicing of colloquial verbs. Next to us sits a young priest. Not even thirty.

He says: 'You don't look local.'

'Oh, no,' I reply. 'I am from far away.'

Nervous awkward silence.

'How is Elefsis these days?'

'Quiet and sleepy, a provincial town without any prospects. Most of the industries are closing down, unemployment, sloth, sin.'

'Has it been so affected by the devastation?'

'We live in a desolate land,' he says. 'This is not our country, we feel we are bystanders in our own home, witnesses of a crime behind glass windows.'

'Any creative responses to this crisis, any ironic distancing from what happens, any sarcasm of the sin?'

'I am afraid that you are a true foreigner,' he sighs. 'Do you know the Greeks or maybe you have forgotten them? The Greeks think of their failure as the failure of the whole world: they cannot accept their specificity. We are prisoners of Plato, unredeemed, against time, irreligious.'

'But you are a priest,' I challenge him. 'Have you done anything to bring these elements to the light of conscience?'

'I cannot do much to remove the burden of a deceptive identity. The only thing I can do is lead the faithful, through the *Iliad* and the *Odyssey,* to the

Bible, make them understand the power of reconciliation, empathy and forgiveness in a society that has chosen violence and falseness as the core principles of its identity. I am young and I know that I have already failed, and that as long as I live that failure will define me.'

He looks in despair towards the silent, vast sky. That is noble, we think, and hopeful. A truck passes by, and the horrible noise does not allow us to say anything. Leaving, he looks back and makes a vague gesture of blessing. At least he knows; yet he follows the wrong direction. Read the Bible first and then move to the *Iliad* and the *Odyssey*: only then the force of identity will be actualised in history. Why do you ignore history and are satisfied with legends and fairy tales? Why has your Church decided to remain a mystery cult from late antiquity, why? But it is too late to ask him. He is gone and I have a visceral aversion towards the cloth.

The bus is coming. Only ninety minutes to reach home.

On the way back. We stop at the other side of the central road again; opposite the monastery, in front of the mental asylum. We take the long pathway to the scary building. The huge white door. We cross the threshold. Recollection: my brother alone in a white room, fed with drugs, disoriented, lost, red eyes, erratic hand movements, reinventing language. The sky is devouring his bed, the clouds are giving birth to snakes, the buildings are digesting human bones, the cars are carrying Attila the Hun and Jesus and certain Mayan kings, the rivers of alcohol are flooding Athens and we are all sinking in an intoxicating ocean of ecstatic self-oblivion: *'I cannot know who I am... I am who I am not...'* We walk slowly up to his room; the door is open, the current tenant is asleep, or unconscious, he looks with his big blue eyes, but he cannot see us, we walk almost hypnotised, in this sanitised white desert, trying to find traces of that departed existence, but nothing is left, his breath, his smell, his absence, they are all gone, so many years later. The ascetic room hatches now a new terrified spirit, also lost, raising his hands towards us, his eyes red and empty, his weak body whiter than the linen, his hands struggling to find a stable point in the invisible world to lean on and perform their cosmic dance. His damaged coarse voice:

'Who are you? Are you the messengers? Are you the angels of the Promised Land? Take me with you, take me home, take me home...'

He falls back in a swoon, breathing heavily, rasping, wheezing, medicated, twitching occasionally, as if he was in some luminous bliss in the hands of angry angels and compassionate demons ... We walk out slowly. The long corridors, the screams, the smell of medication:

'Walk out ... Leave this place, you blasphemous, healthy, sane creatures!'

We obey the angel and we walk out slowly.

The bus is coming; at least public transport works.

'You see,' a man waiting for the bus says loudly. 'After they privatised the bus lines out of Athens, they all run on schedule.'

But we are benumbed and anesthetised; and as we separate, we remember our youth and the James Bond movies we watched together and we talked about them one day before he was gone. I manage to tell him with a broken voice:

'Brother, rest, rest, this country has been unkind to you. She had you destroyed even before you were created, the evil mother, the rotten origin...'

He looks at me with tears in his eyes and silently turns away and ascends to the blue sky above like white smoke. A gale of cold air comes upon me as I am left alone; the doors of the bus close violently and the voice of the driver brings me back to my individuality:

'Look what shits of industrial archaeology they have privatised!'

Day 7

Graffiti around Athens – how can I forget this? I reconstruct the atmosphere of emotions through cries of despair. It goes back in time; when I was studying, my last assignment for my bachelor's degree was entitled *'Obscene Graffiti in the Changing Rooms of the Stadium at Olympia'.* Beyond doubt the continuity of culture in Greece can be proven with the same majestic swear words about body parts, copulation and public abuse about arses since time immemorial. But this is different. They are all over Athens. It is as if freedom of expression has migrated to the walls of the city. Urban folk art and the demotic sublime fused in one.

The current crisis has led to a profound crisis of meaning: nobody trusts the government or the media and the language which consecrates their power. When people appear on television, their voice is framed, distorted and deflected. The city walls capture the majestic irregularity of the colloquial language, its rejuvenating errors, its aggressive irregularities, its ungrammatical configurations. With their quirkiness, they destroy the stability of correct spelling, which makes the alphabetised mind lazy and slothful. They recalibrate semantics because they have to condense expression to its minimal wording. They also know that they are ephemeral: they don't suffer from the heresy of permanence. They recognise their finitude, their evanescence; but they illustrate the unmediated voice of the voiceless, when its language is still boiling.

I have some of them written down:

'Happiness will be our revenge.'

'Public opinion has no opinion.'

'You, where have you been, You?'

'Do not disturb my oblivion.'

'This country is destroyed because of indifference: but do I care at all?'

'I hope nothing, I fear nothing: I am unemployed.'

'If elections could change the system, they would have been unconstitutional.'

'We have become the people who our parents told us never to befriend.'

'Our flag is our shroud.'

'The other half of barbarism is based on your tolerance.'

'Our teaching system is the teaching of our system.'

'Liberate our Time!'

'If god exists, that's his problem.'

I could list more. They are impressive, awkward, badly written, covering big walls, sometimes with colourful images of hallucinogenic properties, illustrating the immense morphogenetic imaginary that lies under the urban streets. They depict the felt history of the present: how the anonymous many, the multitudes, the rabble struggle to maintain their sanity as the whole system implodes and the regular mechanisms of living are derailed.

The graffiti are closer to the heart of the matter than most erudite analyses presented by famous thinkers on television: they show self-criticism ('*Inertia is crude violence*'), deep understanding of political activism ('*Whatever is not overthrown can be destroyed*'), a sense of dignity ('*Happiness will be our revenge*'), the desire to be yourself ('*Your face is a window into chaos*'), a profound sense of the political ('*Freaks of all countries, unite!*'), Kafkaesque surrealism ('*Once a cage went out chasing birds*'), endurance ('*A Laugh will bury them*'), resignation ('*Besides Imperialism, there exists loneliness too*'), pessimism ('*It's better a horrifying end instead of an endless horror*') or even open horizons ('*The most beautiful dreams have no name*').

They are written on walls, of all buildings ('*This is a beautiful wall*', they mock. '*Paint it now again*'). They express the silent rage against a state that has made them anonymous, lost in the confusion of spin and the distorting psychotechnics of the media. In a city without open spaces, walls become inviting pages for the inhabitants to publicise their personal sense of helplessness. Many people are suffering but there is no way that their tragedy can be depicted. It should never find its public representation, it should always remain unstoried. It destroys the archaeological serenity that a historic city without present needs. Prophecies are now written on the walls of the collapsing city, articulating a wild, furious and ominous vision of its inhabitants. It is written by them about themselves. It is a diagnosis of their common atmosphere, of their shared cave of imprisonment. The captives always leave on the walls of their prison signs of how they calculated time so they won't lose a sense of tomorrow.

As I am walking around the centre of the city, a young man is writing something on the wall of the Ministry of Culture, behind the National Archaeological Museum. *'So much democracy we haven't seen since the last dictatorship'.* I am puzzled. I follow him. Further down he writes: *'You cannot imprison our dreams.'* I keep following him.

He spots me:

'What's your problem, jerk?' he shouts.

'Oh nothing, nothing, I am fascinated...'

'Are you with the cops, you, moron?' he carries on with the niceties.

'No, no,' I protest. 'On the contrary, I am from Australia and I am doing some research around the city.'

He changes immediately:

'I have relatives in Melbourne,' he says with a huge smile on his face.

'The whole of Greece has relatives in Melbourne,' I crack the joke. The ice is broken. 'Would you like a cup of coffee?'

'As long as you pay,' he declares, 'I am in.'

We go to the café at the basement of the Archaeological Museum.

Manoly his name, from Crete. He moved to Athens to study when eighteen. He is twenty nine now.

'I wasted five years, he says, of my life in a monastery. Deep down I still believe in god, but in this country, too many churches but no faith, no religion.'

Affinity. My Proustian involuntary memory: I am in a monastery on Mt Athos; it is 1982, I am convinced that I must dedicate my life to the great mystery. I decided to go after that one night: when our professor of Art at the University analysed Goya's *Saturn devouring his children.* I went determined and I left defeated. The mystery lasted less than three months. Watching monks praying, ritualising and fraternising made visible the disintegration of the ultimate question. I keep a copy of Goya's painting with me as the most religious image I have ever encountered. But I must let him talk.

'I didn't have any money, and became a hustler.'

'As everyone does when they cannot find a job,' I mock him.

'Don't ridicule me,' he says. 'I got involved with the wrong people. I became cheap, I stole money, I bashed up people, I raped once or twice, I mixed with the very wrong crowd. I was dying; you know Gogol's *Dead Souls?* Something like that.'

He stops. He wants to talk. Why do I bump onto such interesting people?

'One night, I think in Faliron, we raped, robbed and knocked unconscious a silly and unfortunate transvestite. She was almost dead on the ground, barely breathing. As the others left, I stayed behind because the face reminded of someone I knew. Well, my feeling was true. It was my first cousin; he had helped me a lot when I first moved to Athens. I even owed him money. I was shocked. He only said: 'Manoly, don't say anything to my mother...' It was as if one hundred thousand glasses broke instantly in my heart. I was bleeding, my soul was evaporating, my own body was becoming my punishment. I took him to hospital, gave him normal clothes, washed his face form make-up, threw the wig in the bin, and then called his parents.'

'Well, this is what they call a family saga,' I say in order to lighten up the atmosphere. Coffee comes. Chocolate to be precise.

'I left the next day for a monastery on the island of Evoia. I stayed there for almost two years. Invoking God, supplicating the Virgin, praying to Jesus: regularity, permanence, fixity, fluidity was abolished, eternity was a real experience. The seasons came and went, the rains, the clouds, the desires, the dreams, my old self. I moved to Mt Athos. Iviron Monastery – that huge black hole, unfeeling and unfriendly.'

'You left however.'

'Yes, the monks were insane, obsessed with sexuality and money. Some of them were heavy drinkers. I never talked about any matters of the spirit with them. They accused me of intellectual curiosity, of secular desires, of sloth and other deadly sins. Mean, despiritualised, petty minds ... Totally lost in the narcissism of their certainties.'

'Probably they were doing what they accused you of.'

'To be sure, yes. I have seen them eating like pigs, hiding money like misers and having sex with blond angels from Sweden and giving them in exchange precious old icons – but let's not get into that.'

'So you walked out.'

'I still try to make peace with God,' he says. 'Because I have to make peace with myself.'

'Isn't usually the other way around?'

'No, no. I need points of reference. I need to refer to somebody or to something, which is not me.'

'And what are you doing now?'

'Squatting, in that old building further down. With ten other people. Still looking for that peace treaty with the original ground of being.'

'But why? Are you in a state of war? Why don't you try to understand the *casus belli* before signing your pact of submission? Because you have to submit – you have no option!'

'I know what you mean,' he says. 'It is like the knight playing chess with death in that movie by Bergman.'

'You rebel against the 'system' because of that?'

'It's a mess, mate,' he admits. 'Isn't it? I don't know: some aspects of our self are better to remain incomprehensible. I don't want to project my own personal angst onto the spirituality of my religion.'

'You will be eaten up by anxiety like that,' I say. 'And I'm sorry but I don't think that there is any spirituality in our religion. The privileged position that some pseudo-theologians attribute to the Orthodox faith is due to a deep cultural and political panic. We are so terrified by the modern world that we are unable to admit our defeat; something that is which would have humanised us and would have made us authentic. But the most important part of our self is that we are defeated, humiliated and lost. *My power is made perfect in weakness,* if you remember...'

'I don't know,' he whispers. 'It's a real mess. After the fall, everything is so messy. I am lost, my world is dying, my mind is burning, I have lost all certainties but I won't give up.'

'You overdramatise. Your generation was lucky. You had everything, you could choose: even more, you had the luxury to decline an offer. Do you think that many generations before you had such a privilege?'

'No, no I know,' he says and he is obviously uncomfortable.

I start my attack.

'Some of us worked in factories, restaurants, shops, to make our living. I started working when I was fourteen. We had no option. You wasted time, indulging yourselves as perpetual adolescents, and then you think that you can reclaim and regain it?'

'I was looking for God,' he says in obvious pain. Oh, the fragility of the innocent...

'Can you stop,' I say sadistically, 'this God-stuff? You underestimate history and you want to find God?'

'Why are you so cruel?' he asks.

'Because God is all in all and you cannot see it! The total sum of all things visible and invisible that cannot be reduced to its individual parts. And you cannot see it! And you search for paradises and hells and even more than that, for nothing – although the whole world pulsates with a relentless energy which you should have noticed by now...'

He is confused and lost. He means the best. His heart is in the right place. He is suffering. I remember, I always remember, that great verse by the poet Angelos Sikelianos: *'Oh simplicity, that you cannot recognise your own self...'*

'Alright,' he says. 'You proved my essential banality, the insipid triviality of my being. It's enough. At least I know.'

He is shaking but still smiles. We get up. I pay.

As we separate, he does me the honour.

'Let me show you my latest revolutionary slogan,' he says smiling.

He takes me by the hand, we cross the central street; and we are in front of an old imposing building, opposite the Polytechnic school, a grand hotel in the days of yore, but now, empty, skeletal, without windows. In front of the building, two huge garbage bins. Cats are walking on top. Next to the bins, a bus stop. People wait patiently. Further down are illegal sellers of weird toys.

He takes his spray and writes:

'Keep Athens clean: throw your garbage in Piraeus.' He adds an elegant exclamation mark.

I protest, but it is the performative function of written language that makes us both laugh.

'Oh,' he says, 'The letters of the Greek alphabet! Always ready to make a spectacle of themselves.'

'Good bye, Australian jerk,' he farewells me. 'For your own sake, I hope that you won't find in Athens what you are looking for.'

Polite and straightforward till the end.

Day 8

Omonoia Square again, the Valhalla of our youth. Now inhabited by all the races of the globe, divided into regions, the Somalis, the Albanians, the Georgians, the Nigerians. I have an appointment. It's 5pm, still early, the sun reigning supreme over the dirty square. No hustlers any more, no free and dangerous sex, no prostitutes and pimps. Only drugs, drug-barons and warlords, ready to offer you anything as long as you give them:

'Fifty euros brother and you get the trip of your life...'

'No, I don't want to have any trips...'

'Then run away from this place...' the African man says menacingly. 'Go to the opposite side with the Georgians, they sell girls ... or to the other side, the Albanians sell boys!'

'Your Greek is perfect,' I say.

'Thank you', he replies flattered for being noticed. 'I live here since I was four. Get lost now.'

I move further down waiting for Celèste to arrive, always grand entrance, always late. Suddenly a brawl breaks out, from one side of the square to the other, machetes, daggers and strange long blades appear and the square on the corner of Stadiou and Athenas Streets is splashed with blood. Two policemen are there, supervising the situation from their car; they look amused. I approach one of them.

'You must stop them,' I implore. 'Innocent people are passing by...'

'We are not going to be killed for those cannibals...' one says with contempt and starts laughing.

'Let them kill each other ... It will be easier for us...' adds the other.

I cannot forget their manic laughter. I walk away as the sounds of clashing armies are heard.

Celèste arrives and we move twenty meters down on Athena's street. We enter through an unassuming door and find ourselves in the most lavish and luxurious restaurant I have ever seen.

'These are the secret spots of Athens you must discover,' she says.

Two waiters take us to a table close to the window from which I can still have glimpses of the fight. Clouds appear; it is going to rain.

She says: 'At this very moment, Greek society experiences the panic that overpowers people when they understand that they are not in any way different from others. In anthropological terms, it would be called "imaginative failure" – we lost the creative imaginary to find a symbol for our position in history.'

'What happened? Is an economic collapse a sufficient reason to explain such devastation?'

'Since this state was established, because of some ancient buildings and certain spell-binding texts, the political order convinced or seemed to have convinced everybody that we are different in many substantial ways. But now this foundational principle of self-imposed difference has imploded.Why? Because we became existentially dependent on it. We became afraid to be lost in the anonymity of the many, and thus unable to deal with modernity and with ourselves.'

The food arrives: delicious and cheap.

As we eat, she says: 'We love being archaic, un-modern and un-historical. The Orthodox Church is primarily responsible for this trait, since Byzantium. At a certain stage priests decided to ignore history; at the same time, the state adopted this through the cult of antiquity. So, to use a poetic metaphor, "*we became the admirers*" of antiquity. A culture of perpetual irresponsibility was instituted and thus so many things happen and no one, but absolutely no one can take responsibility about anything.'

'Anything good in this society?' I ask.

'Well, as strange as it sounds, the good thing is that we are less interesting than we think we are. Determined to perpetuate and serve an ancient epiphany, we missed all the new epiphanies which happen every day around us and for us. We became voluntarily blind – probably our blindness is the most significant achievement of our modern culture.'

'We must stop being preoccupied with pathology,' I suggest. 'Tell me something affirmative which might liberate the anxiety of so many beautiful souls.'

'I insist: the best part in us is our insecurity and vulnerability. If we ever realise that, we will cease being parasites. Instead we try to hide everything, disguise it, mask it artfully, until the mask becomes our face and we cannot take it off – which means that we don't have the will to throw it away.'

She pauses, looks at the time on her watch, and adds:

'This is the land of the lotus-eaters, the land of the eternal afternoon. We don't want to go home, we don't want to recognise our self, suspended and apathetic we are drifting hither and thither, nauseous and confused, thinking that all such hyperactivity and agitation is liberty and independence.'

We talk about symbols, landscapes and personalities who influenced and established such confusion, but they all are elsewhere, lost to the immediate experience, prey to nostalgia and to the vultures of confabulation.

'The trauma of the Asia Minor Catastrophe,' she adds, 'the existential vacuum that has never been objectified, rationalised through language, or represented as optical realisation, keeps us down, immobilised by panic, arresting all forms of creative visualisation.'

'Why is memory so crucial in determining contemporary identity, why?'

We cannot answer, so we revert to gossip and small talk. Friendship does not need grand narratives to live on.

After lunch we separate.

'Tomorrow again,' she says, 'at the Acropolis Museum. There is a lovely restaurant up there.'

She adds: 'Don't forget to use the new metro – it is really useful, if they are not on strike, of course.'

It took us almost fifteen days to meet again.

I decide to walk down the Town Hall Square, the old hangout of transvestites and drag queens, a mythical place for artistic hallucinations. It starts raining and a sharp sudden chill covers the city, dark clouds, these strange humid days, aptly called 'air-boiling' in Greek, when you feel that the tipping point of weather is nigh and you must find an umbrella as soon as possible.

As I walk down towards the Monastiraki station, the whole spectacle of the human comedy parades in front of my eyes. At one corner, a man and a prostitute are punching and slapping each other; just a few meters further down two junkies are shooting up in front of everybody. At the next corner people sell guns, together with a *'little sweet sugar, pure sweet sugar!'* Others are shouting in a foreign language at a window just above their head; two prostitutes are smoking hashish, their cheap make-up melting on their face as rain drops fall violently on them.

A young man comes closer: 'Give me two euros,' he tells me with a strange smile. 'I can recite the first rhapsody of the *Iliad* for you...'

'I would prefer the last one,' I retort.

'I haven't reached that part,' he replies, and leaves laughing louder and louder.

I make haste. I have to reach the station before the coming storm. As I am running, images of bodies, faces, hands, cars, trees and clothes mingle into a strange impressionistic painting which envelops everything and I cannot escape its poisonous immoral ecstasy. Heavy and big drops of water start falling – you can hear them, you can feel their weight on your head, Athens is melting, a mist of ominous otherness takes over the streets, Athena's street, the space of my youthful lustfulness. I never looked upwards and the ground rewarded me.

The frenzy just starts. At the Monastiraki station; the old mosque stands by, silent, eternal and minimalistic. And next, the old Christian monastery with strange frescos of the late sixteenth century retouched by Russian style artists in the nineteenth, with the addition of golden lines, silvery decorative motifs and sugary angels. The holy spirit in the form of a deep gray emptiness is surrounded by strong green, blue and red colours, depicting the abysmal dragon with his mouth open, the half-lost face of Jesus, and the sad figure of his mother covered by smoke, burnt candles and salival humidity. The two archangels with their austere and sharp swords have been androgynised by the confused Rococo restorateurs of the nineteenth century, when the Bavarian king arrived to civilise the country.

I notice the strange woman looking after the church, dressed in black, black scarf, shocks and shoes, who comes close to me.

'I dedicated myself to this little church after I lost all my family in a car accident. Twenty four years ago. So much loneliness, but this building talks to me. It tells me stories ... I must tell you some of them.'

'Some other time...' I suggest.

Oh rational thinking, why did I enter this edifice? But the blight is in me, infected by the dark irrationalism of concaved spaces, the wet vaginal feeling of imminent rebirth, the delusion that probably a fragment of sacredness has found refuge in here.

I walk towards the other church of the region, the Kapnikarea chapel.

I have always been in love with this church, only because it stands at the centre of a busy commercial street. In the good old days, it was a great pick-up place of aged wealthy ladies by young gigolos. Today, the street is used by pedestrians and beggars, impromptu artists, dancers, fortune tellers, oriental tea sellers and many more. I walk through them towards the tenth century dark, musty, humid cave. The rain starts falling: it's a storm, it's a really heavy storm. I must go in and stay in for some time.

There are other people huddling in here. As a token of my gratitude I light a candle. I leave five cents simply for the sound effect. But it is the atmosphere, the whispers, the smell of candles, the strong odours of the wet human body, the incense, the priest who reads some prayers over the head of two women, the dim lighting, the frescos, the colours, the chairs – everything: they all tell me to absorb the moment, listen to the rain and forget where I am.

Yet, the silence is broken; not by my own inner voices or by my inability to concentrate. Two women at the small narthex are conversing about the miraculous energies of certain icons.

The first: 'There is no reason for coming to this church. I live here and I know it. *This* icon cannot do anything to heal your migraines.'

The second: 'Where should I go?'

The first: 'You must first go to the monastery of St Ounoufrios. The icon there works miracles. Your migraines will vanish.'

The second: 'I have been there and nothing happened. I also went to Pendeli Monastery and stayed under the icon for a whole night praying – nothing again.'

The first: 'Well, there is only one solution: the monastery of St Irene – you will stay all night under the icon, you will drink the saliva of the Mother of God, and eat the blessed apple. It will work, I guarantee it – you will be healed. The icon in Pendeli works only in possessions and casts out the evil eye. If you had depression you needed something stronger – the icon at the island of Tinos! But, this is nothing ... You will be fine, I am telling you...'

The second: 'I will follow your advice – you know better than I do. But these headaches are really bad. My local priest told me that god gave them to me for my sinful life – because of one affair with a married man years ago!'

'Serious sin, infidelity,' says the other pensively.

'But if God gave me these migraines,' the other asks, 'do you think that the power of these icons is strong enough to change his decision?'

'We will see! The Lord's plans are mysterious...'

The storm is gradually settling down. I must leave the consecrated grounds.

I move towards the ticket box at the train station; in the entrance about thirty people are sleeping on the marble floor covered by blankets. It is around six o’clock. I look carefully and decide to take out my small camera. My lethal voyeurism, the horrible imprint of watching diabolical commercial channels since I was growing up, takes over the best of me. I take two photos when my eyes cross with the eyes of one man on the floor. He looks at me with a strange mixture of rage, contempt and surrender. I cannot move my hands.

His Gnostic gaze nails me down, helpless and speechless – then he starts sobbing louder and louder. ‘Go away’, he says, ‘go away, with your cruel eyes, your sick mind...’ And he keeps sobbing, covering his head with a colourful blanket. I am devastated ... Why did he react so intensely? Did we know each other in the past? The shame of failure? I look around. What is this place? Who am I? No more photos, no more photos...

Association: The whole incident brings to my mind an old story, a guilt of mine which I cannot sublimate. 1983, last year of studies at the University of Athens. My fellow student Hippocrates just comes back from Heidelberg University where he finished his degree in philosophy. Slim, slender, fragile youth, always thinking about existence and being and unconcealment. He is changed; his mind is gone. In its place there was a strange labyrinth of confused words.

‘No more Sartre,’ he is shouting, ‘no more Heidegger, no Husserl, no Hegel – just give me something to eat.’

He vanishes after that meeting; some twelve years later I am walking around the Acropolis' small forest, in a warm summer night when suddenly a white horse with a naked rider on it, a white skinny, vulnerable nudity, totally de-sexualised, totally sacred. People start whispering: *'The existentialist is back'* and I recognise the face of my long lost friend. He looks at me with a strange mixture of rage, contempt and surrender: 'I hate you,' he grunts, 'I hate your balanced mind...' and is lost into the night.

I look around. What is this place? Where am I?

Another disturbance of memory on the Acropolis.

Later the same day, around eight at night. In front of the television – you are taught how boredom becomes interesting.

As Mother and Mrs Felicity are watching the show, I notice that mother is reading the subtitles to her. In the beginning I thought that it is their personal way of communicating but she turned to me and said blushing; 'I am illiterate, I cannot read...' It is the first time I met somebody from her generation who couldn't read.

'I couldn't go to school,' she says.

'Why?'

'After the war, poverty, misery, hunger ... Maybe you think that I am stupid...'

'No, no,' I protest, 'tell me more...'

We forget everything about Suleiman – and the vital history of being unravels.

It is like in a movie by Terence Davies: the silent eye moves with affection and empathy over the shabby and cheap objects of everyday self-definition, the bed, the chairs, the table, the shoes, the clothes, the floor, the wall, the dust, the windows, the dishes, the food-remains. They are sitting next to each other; they whisper, they talk about absence and the significance of being in use.

The two women speak to each other almost in a secret language: something about saints who dismember bodies, or about a lost soul unable to find its way back, or even about a demented patient who died alone in a cold empty hospital room.

'His judgement was given by the way he died.'

They talk with warmth and tenderness about horrible things, about painful disintegrations of the body, the inability to move, strokes, heart attacks, diseases of the bones, cancer, leukaemia, dirty hospitals, sadistic nurses. All they speak about is the senses, the body, the feeling of being abandoned, their hands, their husbands, their homes. They talk about poverty and how:

'Now that everything is lost we must return to the old ways.'

It is an uncanny discussion, full of beautiful dismay, and elemental simplicity.

‘What are you talking about?’ I ask. ‘I cannot understand the language.’

‘This is our own way of not becoming crazy,’ Mrs Felicity says. ‘With words that mean nothing to people like you.’

‘Like me?’

‘Don’t get me wrong,’ she says. ‘I mean to people who haven’t lost anything in their life.’

I must not become defensive.

She continues: ‘We lost so much; and we have been unable to cry and mourn over what is gone. Don’t you understand how much poison we have in our blood? Still we manage to cook and clean and say some good words to each other.’

I am about to make a comment – but Mother shouts:

‘Suleiman is going to destroy a whole city! So much cruelty...’

Horror falls into the room – the atmosphere becomes ominous – even the lights feel the stress, *flick flick flick ...* Are they on strike again?

We turn to the television, the modern grandmother of all archives – terrible fairy tales are depicted there. The event of razing a city to the ground is powerful; the subtitle readings by mother are even more exciting. Suleiman is outside Buda – indeed he conquered Buda and must cross the river to conquer Pest.

Mother reads: 'Suleiman captured the Buda...'

Ms Felicity: 'The Buddha? The god from the east?'

Mother confused replies: 'Well ... Yes. I think so ... Or maybe somebody else?'

Felicity: 'What was he doing there?'

Mother: 'How should I know? Turks can do anything!'

The conversation is hilarious. I cannot stop laughing. More subtitling gems are to come. Interspersed with living fragments of personal history. Mrs Felicity is an individual without ever reflecting about her identity: she has outgrown the circumstances that formed her life.

Graffiti on the wall: '*Euthanase your democracy.*' I love the verb!

Day 9

Before visiting an old friend in Kallithea. I get off the train. In front of the station, many illegal immigrants selling just about anything. Around the corner, a huge supermarket. They have thrown out food, vegetables and bread, some of it just scattered on the road, more food inside the huge garbage bins. Two boys, obviously foreign, are rummaging in them. They have a trolley and throw in whatever they find. I am transfixed. But the drama intensifies: as they jump out, three dogs attack the trolley and them. I witness an incredible struggle between men and beasts. Both sides are hungry and scream and use anything they can to push the other back. People from the nearby windows look – some do not know what to do – others laugh – others close the windows. My nerves, my nerves.

My friend, Thomas, the policeman. I tutored him decades ago, when he was preparing himself for the academy. He failed the exams but he had an uncle on the committee who appointed him anyway – but some formalities had to be kept. The police force? Why? No Freudian reason; if for there is one then it must be for his law studies. Because of Aristotle and Kant: he joined the force on grounds of ethical imperatives.

'Greeks think that they can be free without laws. In reality, they simply walk on the freedom of others. That indifference made me join the force.'

He is married, two children, already in their twenties. His wife Mary, from Alexandria.

Thomas: 'Isn't it sad to accuse the police for everything, as if we are not part of this society? I have seen so many things in my career that you cannot even believe how uncaringly this state operates. The three people who were burnt alive last year and nobody has been charged to this day. The cowardice of those who pretend to be social revolutionaries and never take responsibility: they accuse the structures, the laws and the system, as if they are never here.'

I feel his anger.

'Don't you think that you are a pawn in a game determined by others?'

'No,' he replies. 'What makes you think that my uniform suspends my moral conscience? You, you taught me, years ago, to stand up when we know how to solve a problem.'

Yes, I did.

'I don't agree with the law – but this is the law of the country. We must follow it. And wait till the next elections to change it. Isn't this democracy? But, no, here we have, it's my way or no way!'

Deep breath: 'But ... no! The left think that they are above the law and now the extreme right-wing think that they are the law ... It's the same mentality of those who don't know what freedom is.'

His children have left the family house, indeed have abandoned the country.

'My boy has emigrated to Holland and my daughter is studying to be an actress in London. In a way I am happy for both of them. They left this country and their parents, us, and we have become the orphans. Probably in the new countries, they won't experience the deep sense of despair that has overpowered me recently.'

He is sweaty and anxious.

'I must tell you my dilemma: my gun loaded, in front of me an anarchist youngster with his face covered. I could have shot him dead. I was defending private property and public order. He fell on the ground – he took out a gun. The little shit had a gun! I moved fast and kicked his hand. His gun fell on the ground. I could have killed him, I was on self defence. But I let him go. His eyes were full of horror. I thought of what you had told me: that we all have the right to exist because of our common stupidity. I let him go.' He cries. 'He could have killed me of course.'

Mary comes close and touches his head with both her hands with immense affection. 'I have decided to resign,' he says. 'I will go back to my island. I will start farming again, like my father. This city has destroyed the best in me, my need to believe, my need to belong. I must escape – I am still young, forty five, and there are so many things I can do. I don't want to waste away in yearning and nostalgia for days that I haven't even experienced.'

We have lunch together; his wife is quiet but ubiquitous. 'I just wanted you to know that I remembered everything you told me when I had that youngster on the ground. That we have to choose – and I did.'

There is a compelling innocence around him. As if so much confusion and disorder have remained outside the confines of his existence while in him there is still pulsating a magnetic centre of criminal purity.

I take a taxi and go back home. The driver is polite and talkative.

'How can I come to Australia,' he asks.

'You must fulfil certain criteria.'

'But can we come in through the back door?'

'Very unlikely,' I say.

'And you must be less than forty years old. I am fifty! Can't you help?'

'No, I cannot.' Silence.

As we move along Syngrou Avenue, we suddenly see a strange creature half-man half-woman, dressed in black tight clothes, jumping in front of us. He starts dancing and takes his clothes off one by one. His lean and toned body shines in the afternoon. Yet he keeps dancing. He is left with satin underwear and nothing else. A police car passes by and one man from them shouts:

'Keep shaking your ass, Lady Gaga...'

They go away beeping their horn and shouting. The driver turns to me and says:

'Look, how much madness each one of us can carry within himself ... There is no salvation, my friend, no escape. Either in Australia happy or unhappy in Greece, the same madness prevails within us...'

How can I fit this man, my policeman student, to the general scheme of things in his own country? Recently, after an avalanche of negative criticism against the police force, a woman silently held up a small banner with the inscription: *'Policemen have mothers too!'* She was reacting to attempts to justify the rebellious youths with guns, who robbed banks in order to fund their revolutionary struggle, on the basis of their upbringing: the mother of one of them had witnessed her father killing a friend of his with a hammer, and then her father's own suicide. Greeks have a strong fear of difference: anything different from them increases their insecurity, their self-doubt: but what are they doubtful about?

Between their own Scyllas and Charybdes, they manage to achieve a precarious temporary balance – a few moments of tranquillity and rest, which are only too ephemeral. Soon the extremities of history find them again: invasions, civil wars, financial collapses and the cycle starts over again. What they thought of as solid ground is suddenly discovered to be on the verge of a volcano. It starts shaking and trembling, so their perception is blurred and their reactions become frantic.

In a minute, whatever they thought as good becomes threatening; friendly, it becomes alienating; reassuring, it becomes lethal – they start screaming and yelling, attack the people who try to make them think rationally and then ransack all supermarkets buying anything that could help them survive the upcoming famine.

They haven't forgotten the famine of 1943 under the Germans. In 1987, when one of the usual war alerts with Turkey took place, Mother bought twelve kilos of bread, twenty kilos of rice, fifteen cartons of long-life milk, twenty kilos of spaghetti, immense quantities of consumables half of them with already past their expiry date with the other half expiring in several weeks. The bread moulded a few days later, the milk became undrinkable and everything else had to be thrown out after those pernicious Turks decided (fancy that...) not to carry out their plans to drill for oil in the Aegean Sea.

Who won? The supermarket owners who sold everything that they had to dispose of. But Mother was very happy for several days:

'We won't die of starvation, at least...' she was saying. 'We will die of something else but not of starvation...'

This is my short dialogue with Mrs. Felicity later that night.

'I am illiterate, as you know, but what gave me the feeling of being myself was the voice of my auntie who was reading to me the Arabian Nights, when I was a child. All those names, Scheherazade, Haroun, Ali-Baba, Alladin and so many others made me feel so good, so Greek, so ... How can I say it, so human ... You are a learned man – can you tell me why?'

'Probably because they are so romantic,' I reply stupidly.

'Maybe,' she says hesitantly. 'But ... no, no!' she concludes emphatically. 'It is because they give me a feeling of wonder so that I am never suspicious of other people. It sounds bad what I am going to say but I have only gratitude in me – even for my misfortunes. I learned something through them.'

I become very sentimental when I am confronted by authenticity.

Day 10

Early meeting with George. Eight in the morning in front of the University. Sunday. Oh yes, the University of Athens, unforgettable, youth without redemption, with frustrated yearnings and misplaced ideas.

I went early (nostalgic sentimentalism, I would say) and waited. Looked around, morning stillness, eerie urbanity. I notice a number of strange tents between the central building and the Academy. Refugees are sleeping between the sparse bushes around the prestigious edifices. Middle Eastern or African – one of them got up and in front of everybody defecated thickly around the trunk of an olive tree – the morning ritual of universal liberation. Others watching, started urinating as if that was the most natural thing to do early in the morning. At the very heart of the city.

George appeares, late as always.

'Let's go to Thission for coffee,' I say.

We start walking down Coraes Square and towards the old city. There in the middle of the street, five minutes away from the stinking abodes of high education, a miracle, a transfiguration. The street is closed to cars as twenty children from a school nearby stage an enchanting performance of Aesop's myths. I sit down.

The teacher is reading the texts and the children are commenting loudly:

'What should we do to the fox?' she asks.

'Let her go to her mother,' shout most children. Other children look displeased and insist that the fox should be punished severely.

'Animals should not behave like that...' says one blond beast ten years old. Finally they agree: 'Fox go home! Your mother is not amused with your behaviour.'

We talk about so many insignificant issues, like national identity, religious faith and political ideologies, for one hour, which means we are both bored with each other. He makes the first move and says that he has to go home. I decide to walk down towards Monastiraki. As I turn around the corner of the old gas factory, I find myself in the middle of the most spectacular oriental bazaar. I have never seen it before – something between Teheran and Lahore, enveloped by oriental music and glued together by many languages. Roma women and girls dancing for money, musicians from Caucasus, Iraqi singers, people from all over the east selling anything, from computers to pepper, from Persian carpets to digital clocks made in China. It takes me hours to make my way through this magnificent colourful extravaganza that totally immerses me in a world of anxious and restless otherness. I start walking alone, aimlessly.

As I move towards Thission the inexplicable enigma of the Acropolis emerges. An elderly woman tells me in broken Greek pointing with her finger:

'That white building ... eaten many peoples...'

I know ... I know ... It's not even white, anyhow...

Glorious sunshine around, soft soothing breeze – you can hear the constant humming of a chaotic enthno-genesis although you can make no sense of what is said.

Give me open spaces and I will make new temporalities...

But then again: I confess, *mea culpa, mea maxima culpa,* my blasphemous secret. Well ... you know... I must spit it out – okay, here it comes: I never liked the Acropolis! Since the very first time I visited the rock I felt cold and distant from its visible and invisible grandeur. Perhaps because the school excursion was always to the *'Sacred Rock,'* I always felt that it was my duty to like and venerate the building. I was twelve when I dared tell the teacher, a Cretan of immense proportions and of great pedagogical skills:

'But, Sir ... hmmm, hmm, this is just a heap of stones ... It is an unlivable space...'

I have never forgotten the thunderous slap on my face that threw me to the ground...

'Sacrilegious little shit,' he shouted. 'These stones made us what we are...'

I was on the ground, tears in my eyes and I couldn't reply.

And I still cannot understand how stones can give identity to my personal insignificance. Five years later, he is gone, we have a better teacher, with a sense of humour and literary tastes. One of my fellow students asks the most abominable question of all:

'Missus, who changed this building into a summer shop?' (Meaning what happened to its roof since all summer shops are roofless.)

She laughs and we all laugh.

'I think either the Turks or the Venetians ... They were claustrophobic and loved being exposed to the fresh air of Attica...'

'What were they doing up here?'

'It's because of the view – foreigners love exotic views!' she replies, laughing constantly. Her words give me the opportunity to look around and discover the panorama of chaotic uniformities that comprise the modern city. Meanwhile the same teacher gives me the first volume of Marcel Proust's *In Search of Time Lost.* Its reading makes me never look at the Acropolis again, except in photographs. Enough with these ruminations.

Straight back home. Mother is waiting. Sunday afternoon.

'Let's go to the movies,' I suggest. 'An old movie,' I added.

'Which one?' she asks.

'*The Ogre of Athens!* It is on around five at the Cine Club.'

'By taxi?'

'No worries.'

After the 2004 Olympics taxis can be found in abundance; I remember the days when you were at the mercy of the driver, who could opt not to take you, because you were going to the direction he didn't want to go. Now they are polite, friendly and must issue receipts. Actually they give you the receipts that others left behind!

The cinema is in Amerikis Square, thirty minutes from home. Up Piraeus Street, through the centre of Athens. We pass by the School of Polytechnic where the notorious student rebellion took place in 1973. What happened is another story and, as history is learnt through its inaccuracies, the incident has been transformed into the career spinner for a generation of illiterate politicians, devoid of skills, education or expertise. They participated in the so-called 'resistance' against the dictatorship of 1973 – in spirit or in deed; but they all deserve to be materially rewarded for their heroism and eternal spirit of rebelliousness. The mythology of bullshit heroism has elevated these greedy nobodies to untouchable political celebrities. So, they steal money, they usurp positions, they ridicule democracy, and they are still luminous symbols of resistance and rebellion.

With them, it is obvious: Greek society remains an Ottoman formation, it hasn't de-Ottomanised itself, and because of such mercenaries, it will never do so. But hey, stop with your unfair negativity: we have democracy because of them! No, we don't! Definitely not because of them! The fairy-tales concocted about that building have destroyed the innocence of true believers; it has been transformed into a symbol of opportunism and, after the Parliament, is the second most despised space in the country.

We arrive ten minutes before it starts. No more realism now: we enter the universe of Greek expressionism, as Nikos Koundouros imagined and instituted it back in 1955. The film is the most important testimony to the dark, secret and arcane society, unable to deal with itself, its duplicities, its dissimulations, its insincerities. It starts. The silence of all viewers sets the tone – and then the black and white magnificence explodes on the screen. Shadows move, shadows talk, angular shapes and pointed sharp objects cut through the anxieties of a society that is struggling to regain balance.

Mother of course looks around: 'Lovely cinema,' she says. Huge air conditioning pipes protrude like gigantic lion heads. 'It's a pity we cannot smoke.' 'Can you be silent?' whispers someone from the back seats. I am curious – but she doesn't show any interest for the movie. She looks around, touches the velvet upholstery, looks back and then again at the walls, which are decorated with portraits of famous movie people. 'Who is that woman?' she asks.

'Jeanne Moreau.'

'Beautiful woman...'

'And that man?'

'James Cagney...'

'Oh, he is handsome...'

'Mum, could you shut up ... I am trying to watch the film...'

'And that blond one?'

'Jean Harlow.'

She doesn't respond until the scene when the underworld figures choreograph their infernal life. She looks transfixed, full of curiosity and involvement. She says: 'This is how it was, some many decades ago, when we were terrified and hungry.' The voices from the screen are chanting Vedic hymns to the unknowable chthonian gods under their feet: *'I have my little brother seriously sick in hospital. Jesus, help me, to finish this job. With the money I will be his doctor!'* Their feet thumping again and again against the walls that separate the worlds, they moan and sigh and groan and keep beating their heads against the invisible fortifications around their solitude – another one squeals: *'I need only a taxi to make my living – it will be enough!'* as if he is the Pythian oracle announcing scrambled messages to tell the world that a new era is coming close and everything will be new again, the Celestial Athens of our most secret desires will rise up from its Atlantic desolation and will sing again: *'Oh, ich, ach, the sun has set in our heart!'* and the chorus will respond: *'Oh God , look how gallantly they die!'* and the antiphonal sonorities will reach their crescendo with their own apocalyptic evangelism: *'We have a doomed destiny we have a damned faith: life is bitter and our death is bitter – what to choose?'* Tragedy again.

They dance, no: they dig, they sing, no: they visualise – who are they? Shadows on the screen, shadows of forms bygone yet they make us restless and uncomfortable and sad.

I feel that mother's nails have almost cut my skin as she is herself in panic:

'Let's go out of here,' she says sobbing. 'This film gives me the jitters and I won't sleep tonight.'

But the film ends and the proof of its success sixty years after it was made is that we all leave the theatre in silence, almost in reverence, with immense and mighty contrition.

Day 11

Television is banned during my stay: no more visual poison. Yet Mother always turns it on around eight. 'News Time,' she announces. I always move to the other room. However, you cannot disregard or ignore the voices that come out of that machine. They are the same in all channels, saying the same things about the same issues. They are all happy.

One of them, the most disgusting and successful, who purchased another name because he couldn't stand the banality of his own, talks mellifluously. He announces: '*The fact that my wife has an annual income of six million euros has nothing to do with my political career and doesn't in any way privilege me against any other candidate. I am here to serve the nation.*'

They all agree; even his opponents.

'*Nobody ever made any allegations against you!*' one says.

The other insists: '*We don't do criticism ad hominem!*'

The third goes even further: '*You political contribution corroborates this – money is irrelevant!*'

The day that the earth will stand still is around the corner. You don't know these people, my good readers, and it's better not to. This creep (Fouché plus Talleyrand plus Vyshinsky, wrapped in one) is the legal mastermind who concocted the following judiciary practice: he established the legal framework through which any crime, unlawful act or simple misdemeanour by a politician is exculpated even before it is committed.

I beg her: 'Can you change the channel?'

She does: another group of politicians screaming and yelling at each other. We cannot understand a word. Another channel.

Finally we are at the station of the Greek parliament.

A rather large, chubby and well-fed gentleman has the floor; he is coming up with serious allegations.

'Yesterday evening, five, I repeat *fiiiiive,* unidentified airplanes appeared in the sky over Thessaloniki. (He stops; he is angry, he is very angry, he is sweating.) What were they doing over the capital of Greek Macedonia? (He knows the answer.) They were *spraying,* yes, ladies and gentlemen, they were *spraying* the population with toxic gases! (He is screaming now.) *The spraaaaaaayings must end immediately!* The toxic skies theory is true! These are chemical trails planned to cause sterilisation and population control! They must stop *nowwwwww!* (Applause from members.) How were these airplanes flying? (Yes, how?) By forming with their trails the shape of the Star of David! (His body is shaking!) Yes, yes, we know who ... (He stops here full of innuendo ... his finger on his forehead...) who want to cause mental instability to the Greeks so they can control them ... (He breathes deeply, he bangs his fists on the desk and yells with belligerent decisiveness). Well, *noooooooooooo,* the Greek race and its spirit will fight back and will destroy the intruders! (He is really ecstatic...) We shall triumph, ladies and gentlemen, because the God of Greece is Greek...' He is crying. *'Stop the spraaaaaaayings now!'* he shouts as he leaves the stage.

Thanks to the great architect of the universe a blackout takes place, since the electricity union is on strike again; during the absence of such sonic pollution, meaning is restored to the world. It lasts only twenty minutes, darkness, black stillness, bliss, the saving grace of the ground less void. No voice interferes with our thought processes. Some candles make this wretched reality roman tic and spooky. Only during these moments do we seem to be happy and content and ourselves.

The magic doesn't last long: electricity is back and human voices return us to nullity.

Final stroke: from the same channel. I tune in because in fifteen minutes they will screen a program on koalas and I get very emotional about these vicious creatures, especially when I travel.

Scenes from an opera buffa: an ex-minister of finance, one of the most stupid gardeners of the previous prime minister explains full of fury and narcissism that he had received a very important document in electronic form from France, but he lost it.

'I left it somewhere on my ministerial desk,' he shouts at the members of the committee who question him; *'I could not find it. What do you want me to do? I lost it.'* He bangs his hands on the desk, he yells at a member of the committee and he leaves as if he was in a café.

I turn to the newspaper. No more images, no more moving shadows – words words words, only, please! Oh yes, here we go again. After a minister of the previous government left his office, they found on his desk the most notorious document, which encapsulates the quality of all public servants in the country. On a single loose sheet of paper, written by the hand of a man who presented himself as the pillar of rectitude and advocate of meritocracy, less than ten words say it all: *'He is good for nothing: just squeeze him anywhere you can.'*

Finally, another one, the epitome of the Peter Pan syndrome, declared on national television: *'I was only a minister between the years 2006 and 2009. I was not aware of the financial situation. I swear it in the name of my personal honour.'* He had spent seventy two thousand euros on neckties alone. It is both comical and repulsive – a gay man pretending to be un-gay, since the nation cannot accept gayness. The nation, yes the nation, which was governed by a homosexual prime-minister and president of the republic for twenty odd years – and no macho heterosexual ever dared raising the issue.

Greek language has a long history; in the medieval period, politicians, the politicals to be precise, was the name given to prostitutes. Actually prostitutes have a story to tell – whereas these rejects of life can only destroy stories.

Day 12

Walking aimlessly, you discover. Piraeus has a harbour and that you can take a boat to the islands and come back the same day. Let's go: Syros, Paros or Naxos? No, too far away. Alright then some where closer; Spetses. Just for one day. The sea, the sea, blue, mesmeric and inviting. You simply spend all your time watching the shades of blue, inter acting with clouds, birds and boats. The islands appear suddenly, gray and treeless rocks. I look around and admire the transparency of space; there are so many things in between but every thing can be seen through the other, glowing and waiting.

Stray thought: Lawrence Durrell talked about 'the mild poetry' of the Aegean Islands; others talk about 'their rough physicality.' Let us talk about their lived experience.

'Don't buy this spaghetti dish,' the restaurant man says. 'It is too much.' He is right. 'Order the local fish delicacy.' He is right. 'Also have this local cheese – cheap and delicious.' He is right. There is something wrong with these people here. They tell you the truth, are sincere and do not shout. Having been totally destroyed by the hermeneutics of suspicion, this pernicious sincerity undermines my very intellectual foundations.

The lady at the ticket office suggests: 'It is unfair to sell tickets at this price now. Why don't you come back in two hours, when the price will be halved, according to availability?'

That's really diabolical – they are all so good.

But good moments never last. The restaurant is located at the small harbour, overlooking the narrow sea with the boats. From afar you can see Poros and the other side of the Peloponnese. As I am enjoying the spaghetti, content, smiling and absent-minded, sound and fury takes over the place. Sound and fury, well is an understatement – something serious is happening. Two men are punching each other; others try to separate them but the fight is soon generalised. From what I gather the owner of the restaurant next to this one didn't want to issue a receipt to a customer. The law says that if receipt is not issued, the customer has the right not to pay at all. That's what happened. Soon the police arrive. In their attempt to quash tax evasion, the government sends not only the tax police but also the normal police squad. The brawl becomes total. Other restaurant owners start fighting back, they call their friends and families, they start pushing back the police who do not know what to do. Soon the member of parliament elected by the Left opposition arrives. He starts inciting them to overthrow the odious regime imposed by the Germans and their troika; he tells them that they don't have to issue receipts because the greatest thieves are the Greek state and the Germans, and that police terrorism will not be tolerated. The whole harbour is up in flames, metaphorically and literally. Soon they push the police back towards the narrow alleys and since they are only six or seven men they succeed in confining them at the police station. The People's Police take over. The official police are locked in, their electricity is disconnected and the water supply cut. The media soon arrive. Local television, radio and the rest. I just wanted several hours of peace and a good spaghetti – now look what happens...

Meanwhile, the whole island is up in arms. Some forcefully denounce the oppression, the exploitation and the terrorism that the state imposes upon them. Black flags are raised over houses. Some remember the German Occupation, when they confiscated all the food supplies.

'We will end up starving and dying like flies, like back in the terrible winter of 1942,' lament the older ones. Others remember the glorious days of national pride and independence during the eighties, when the country was purely Greek! *'Greece belongs to the Greeks!'* More slogans are shouted from every direction: *'Law is the right of the working class,' 'People, you are starving, why are you not fighting?' 'Terrorism will not be tolerated.'*

Everything is out of place, bizarre and surreal.

Soon helicopters with more police arrive; even army squadrons from Athens and other islands. The whole siege lasts over five hours. The policemen from the station are freed. Heavy presence of armed guards everywhere. I haven't even finished my spaghetti and the fish is now cold and soggy. Time to go. They spoil the supper of an emigrant simply for a piece of paper?

The flying dolphin appears. I jump in and don't look back. Oh the sea, the sea...

Day 13

Athens, again. The decline is obvious. The optimism around the Olympic Games of 2004 is completely for gotten. Yet obsessions die hard:

'If we leave the Euro-zone,' a friend says, 'the whole of the European Union will disintegrate!'

I walk through the main street in front of the School of Polytechnic. Many shops closed, empty buildings, burnt buildings, abandoned buildings. Further down, in front of the Polytechnic, drug traffickers, male hustlers, female prostitutes, pimps, and social activists fighting for liberation from the bourgeoisie.

The activists protect the *'Sacred asylum of the university'* against any police invasion; inside the building, as well as in its surrounding areas, drug traffickers are selling their kind of paradise.

'As long as the police stay out, freedom prevails on the academic grounds of the institution!' my old communist friend declares emphatically.

'What about the drug dealers?' I dare ask.

'They are not as bad as the capitalist state which imposes poverty, misery and exploitation on the people!' he continues with more bravado.

'We have succeeded in keeping the cops out,' he brags pompously. 'The fight to overthrow neo-liberalism will continue for a long time. Greece is the weakest link in the chain of capitalism. The revolution will begin soon. There will be victims but socialism will triumph at the end.'

'Who will win?'

'Us, the people, the people will be in government with us and through us.'

'Haven't we heard that before?' I ask.

'With us it will be true this time!'

He is happy, and certain and in full flight.

'Let's walk,' I urge. He agrees. We move towards the National Archaeological Museum. Between the Polytechnic and the Museum there is a small pedestrian street. In the late seventies and early eighties, it used to be a hub of spontaneous cultural happenings, performances, music bands, poetry readings as well as risqué events, like drag queen shows and homosexual activism. Now it is full of homeless people, junkies, mafiosi, pimps, prostitutes, thieves. Garbage, stench and filth everywhere.

'Where are the police?' I ask.

'We don't allow them.'

'Why?'

'Because they represent capitalism!'

'What about criminality?'

'They must live also,' he pontificates with his figure pointing at me. 'They react to the alienation and the exploitation they suffer under the neo-liberalist memorandum that Germany has imposed upon us.'

'But they are exploited by drug barons to make money, and be sold at the meat market.'

'Yes ... but ... They are only petty low life, lumpenproletariat, nothing dangerous. And anyway they are not used by capitalists, the big sharks who devour honest working people...'

Then he bursts into a tirade against me: 'Have you turned neoliberal now? Do you accept the policies of the capitalist state that exploits, destroys and impoverishes our people? Do you accept police intervention and brutality? The German memorandum of control and subordination?'

He is already thirty five. He hasn't worked a single day in his life. He hasn't finished his degree. He will never finish his degree. He is paid by his political party to be an agitator. He goes everyday to all university institutions around Athens, waiting for any incident that can be used against the police, the state, capitalism, neo-liberalism, Friedrich Hayek, Milton Friedman, the American imperialists en masse, and so many other demonic spirits that populate the air of planet earth, especially over Greece. He is furious with me now.

'Read Naomi Klein's *The Shock Doctrine!* Arm yourself: the revolution is near and it will be full of blood!'

He keeps pontificating, pointing at me with his finger which is, really, symbolic violence.

'You know what happens all over the planet by the counter-offensive of neoliberal conservativism.'

'What makes you think,' I ask, 'that you are progressive?'

'The legacy of Marx and Lenin!' he gloats. 'Also, Slavoj Zizek's belief that the revolution will start from Athens! We must fight back, cease being the guinea pigs of neoliberal fascism ... There will be blood ... We will kill reactionaries ... We will rebuild socialism with the assistance of South American countries, like Venezuela and Argentina! Cuba will also help!'

I have to go. I am sorry. You must be on something. I run away and do not look back.

I walk alone towards Victoria station. I am going to meet my professor, from the university days, back in late seventies. On the way, I come across the other tertiary institution, the School of Economics. I cannot recognise the place. Garbage, litter, rubbish, junk, even faeces scattered all over its narrow courtyard.

'Why don't you clean it?' I ask.

'We want to show the filthy face of capitalist education,' one student tells me.

'It is not hygienic,' I dare add.

'There is no health in capitalism!'

As I look around, I see homeless people lying on the ground, with food scraps all over them, dirty, with handmade hasish pipes, some of them naked, others pissing in front of everybody, one of them is masturbating, another is covered by a blanket covered with mud. Students walk between them, as if they are not there.

At the entrance, poor foreigners are selling cheap Chinese products, thin, weak, emaciated creatures. They are ready to pack their merchandise and enter the building. The police cannot enter, so we can admire the ironic spectacle of both looking at each other through the railings, less than five fingers away from each other.

I stop a taxi. I have seen enough resistance against capitalism and neo-liberalism for one day.

Finally, my professor of days past. We meet at the usual café. Hippocratous Street. So many intellectual debates have taken place here since time immemorial. The coffee was and still is dreadful – and expensive. The chairs particularly uncomfortable.

'Well,' he says, 'you must have seen enough by now. The spectacle of a declining Athens is not monumental or tragic. It is only distressing.'

'Indeed heart-breaking,' I add.

'You see, it happens,' he continues, 'because we tried to immobilise time – we didn't want to work with time; consequently we lost all sense of direction.'

'Who are these we? Everybody here says "we" because they avoid personal responsibility. I never try to do it myself. Did you?'

He becomes austere and didactic.

'I know that metaphors are not sufficient to describe such complex situations. But we are Athenians, my old student, unfortunately Athenians, what else? We can only suggest political interpretations...'

'Then tell me then: who are these "we"?'

'The political order that prevailed.'

'Who elected them?'

'Some of us,' he consents sadly, 'but not all of us.'

'Then who is to blame?'

'All of us: neither exactly guilty, nor exactly innocent.'

'And what did it happen then?'

'We were skilfully isolated from the rest of the world; we accepted the idea of being an exception, some sort of singularity. All intellectuals struggled to impose a way of thinking that perceived this country as an aggregate of privileged minorities – a broken nationality, fragmented into politicised clans and party-like extended families. The conflict established an introverted and inward looking mindset, unable to deal with external realities and thus confront the invincible flow of modernity. When external challenges appear, we turn inwards like snails and refuse to deal with them. We are the ultimate outcome of generalised sterility.'

'Nobody reacted?'

'Nobody could react. By isolating ourselves we lost any sense of comparison. We couldn't correlate and consequently we couldn't relate. Thus we completed our flight into nothingness.'

He breaths heavily, he is in pain, his diagnosis is not the product of smugness but of personal mutilation. He adds:

'We must now translate this situation into an ethical vocabulary of action. Hubris is born out of the inability to start a dialogue with others – hubris, the permanent temptation of all nations left behind by history. We don't have myths, tragic myths, to confront our own delusions. So, we celebrate a world of non-sequiturs which has become the best world for us, a heap of illusions elevated to the status of a foundational myth.'

'What is to be done?'

'Discover the terror of the real, descend to the uncertainties of freedom and the moral scandal of democracy – all of which, under the circumstances, will be catastrophic.'

'Democracy – what a Greek concept and what an un-Greek practice...'

'It is true. We did everything unworthy of us. For thirty five years we have a democracy ruled by non-democrats and administered by several privileged dilettantes who find it exciting and enthralling to experiment with every possible scenario about the future of this society.'

'And after they fail, they simply leave.'

'Do you remember some verses by the most important political thinker of our history, C.P. Cavafy?'

'Cavafy, a political poet?

'More than you think ... He is the only one who understood politicians because he didn't have a theory about politics ... Listen to these verses: "*...he dressed quickly and escaped ... /performing just like an actor/who, once the play ends,/changes costume and departs.*" This is what our politicians have been.'

I love listening to the rhythmic patterns of Cavafy's irregular idiom.

'They depart by changing their mask and their role. As I said, right now we experience our private and collective flight into nothingness. Finally! We enter the European twentieth century. Now, we experience the post World War I nihilism – our philosopher is Oswald Spengler, at last! Shallow and accurate, simplistic but fundamental!'

'What are we going to find in nihilism?'

He smiles: 'Probably our better self, my good student ... Everything we rejected ... Everything we thought was not us but is at the core of our existence...'

It is late in the afternoon, he is sad, resigned and melancholic: there is a drama in him that transcends the limitations of his personality. The coffee is still undrinkable and the chairs so uncomfortable, my backbone suffers gravely by my awkward contortions to find the proper position.

Evening, another film: Alekos Alexandrakis' *The Suburb of Dreams.* There was a time when films were made only because some people felt the need to give voice to those who were lost and image to those who could not be seen. Alexandrakis, an actor, made this film by himself back in 1963. Its story is about how two petty thieves are planning to steal the money that an elderly woman hides under her bed. But after they break into her house around midnight, they find her dying of a heart attack; yet, instead of stealing the money and leaving her behind, they call for an ambulance and save her life. *'Don't worry, old granny,'* they say. *'We will look after you ... You will get better...'* They leave without taking the money; happy because they did the right thing and ashamed because they were so unfair.

The film is simple, uncomplicated, romantic. It has no pretensions, it reveals no secrets, it is not even aware of its formal construction. It gives magnificent shots of flowers surrounded by squalor and dirt, of silly dreamers immersed in the sordidness of their home and the misery of their neighbourhood, it constructs antinomian images of guilt and innocence, remorse and naivety, of anxiety and community.

As you watch it, time is suspended – you are in the presence of something that despite the years has maintained its energy and force. It also does something more: it reveals the reality of the anonymous heroes who are tempted by evil but yet they always chose to do the right thing. They nurture a moral vision of life. They have an invisible centre and they drift around without ever being lost: they don't need rescue, as they are not suffering for recognition. They are grateful because they are here and relate and converse and can take care of their flowers. Their love for the useless and the unusable makes them civilised and interesting. Their life is not determined by their needs but their needs by their life. I have met them – they are still around and they will rise up – these are our famous men ... They made us romantic and idealistic and generous, from within their own self unawareness...

Really, it is strange what a movie can do...

But the night is not to end with such sublime emotions. After the film, I take a taxi to go home. The driver is rather uneasy.

'We must follow the other way to Piraeus, because there is a huge rally around the centre of the city by the Enraged Citizens.'

I get suspicious. He wants to take me the longest possible way so that he will get more money.

'No,' I insist, 'can you take me through the centre. We can go down Piraeus Street and then drive straight all the way.'

'I am telling you,' he insists. *'It is not safe.'*

'I will get another cab,' I say. 'Go that way otherwise I am getting off.'

'Ok,' he says in resignation. 'I didn't make any money all afternoon. But *you* will regret it.'

I should have followed his advice. He lives and works here: I should have shown more respect.

As we slowly move through the city, I reflect: Athens is an ugly city, the epitome of architectural malformation. But its ugliness vanishes at night. Then all its buildings develop the intentional uniqueness of their maker that transforms them and makes them glow with the aura of their isolated individuality. All of them together under the sharp light of the day dissolved into an aggressive mass of incoherent jumble. At night, they separate, they gain particularity, they stand one by one, odd, quirky, interesting – you look at them and you see individual cases, specific forms, significant particularities.

These are my musings as we drive through a central street. Then, unexpectedly, we see people running frantically up and down, with their faces covered in balaclavas, throwing stones, bricks and anything they can get their hands on against the police force standing on the opposite side of the road. Cars are blaring, police sirens, ambulance sirens, obscene words, gun shots, more obscene words, tear gas canisters, more and more obscene words: the whole pandemonium of a typical confrontation with the anarchists in front of us. The eternal Greek political folk-lore.

'I told you we should have gone the other way...'

I don't know what to say ... silence...

'I am sorry...' I mumble...

But now, we must escape. A traffic policewoman appears and instructs him to follow the other street – but she adds melancholically:

'I am afraid you are trapped ... Find some back streets for cover...'

And trapped we are. And that's what I witnessed.

Many youngsters with balaclavas appear, police men are running after them, the youngsters are setting garbage bins on fire, throw Molotov bombs against shops, break the windows of many others, destroy banks and ATMs with hammers, break car-windows, marble floors, marbled walls, kiosks, or anything that gets in their way. Some others get into the open shops and steal whatever they find. I can see with my own eyes a number of them emptying a shop selling sun glasses – one says to the others:

'Gucci and Versace glasses for your girls, motherfuckers ... Death to capitalism...'

They all laugh...

As they rush out with the loot in their hands, pockets and backpacks, they start throwing pieces of marble or stones against everybody, while still joking and sneering and making obscene gestures to the very few shop-owners who try to defend their possessions. I see one old man sitting down in front of his looted shop and hitting his head with his hands crying loudly like a child. Another one, who was obviously inside, tries to extinguish the fire by pouring water from plastic bottles while moaning like a wounded animal. To this day, I cannot forget that anguished moaning...

The young revolutionaries, 'the kids who feel the need to express their anger' keep throwing stones and Molotov bombs against all directions. One stone hits the back of the taxi.

'Holy mother of god,' the driver shouts. 'They will ruin my taxi and it's the only thing I have to feed my family.'

He hasn't finished his sentence and a huge brick falls just on the front of the vehicle. He starts swearing, and turns the car around a street as fast as he can.

'Fucking anarchists,' he grunts angrily. 'They have a lust for destruction, without thinking of people like us, struggling to make our daily bread. Am I a capitalist? Am I wealthy? I have been working since I was fourteen and I bought this taxi ten years ago ... I have nothing else to live on...'

He shouts, swears and screams abuses from his window at them. Behind us we can still hear the pandemonium, explosions, breaking glass, car exhausts, angry voices. He turns around another street, and then again and again, he knows where he is going, but I feel lost. I vaguely remember this part of the city where I spent the most adventurous days of my youth.

We find ourselves behind a central square, at a narrow alley, very close to the clashes, from where we can see the back side of imposing neoclassical buildings on fire, majestic and venerable buildings, burning into bright flames and black smoke. We cannot move. But we think that we are safe here. He switches off the taximeter. We remain silent, as a whole block can be seen burning. We are shocked.

'Look at that building. It must be the old cinema ... *Atticon!'* He says pointing with his finger. 'I spent my whole youth in there ... All my money to watch films every weekend ... Now look! Ashes, smoke, charcoal ... by the Greeks themselves...'

Silence. We can hear the greedy mouth of fire swallowing the chairs, the big curtain, the wooden boxes – our youth, our need for awe and wonder, our embodied memories. The smell of burnt fabric feels to me like burning flesh, the flesh of our dreams, our idealism, our enthusiasms. Now all gone up in smoke because of the need of some bored bourgeois youths to express their fury against the system built up by their parents...

The fire squad appears, more sirens again, people from their windows at the opposite side start yelling in despair, and some with tears:

'The *Atticon* cinema is burning ... The oldest cinema in Athens ... Fucking anarchists!'

It is a sad spectacle. Over the buildings in front of us, we can see a hypnotic blaze against the black sky of the night. We live our own little apocalypse but we cannot say a word – all noises come from very far away, all movement is in slow motion, all distance is magnified.

Suddenly, two people in balaclavas appear; they are holding stones in a bag and if I can see correctly a bottle, which looks like a Molotov bomb. The driver cannot control himself and jumps out of the car, furious, wild, feral.

'You want to burn everything down you fucking bastards, do you? My taxi too? Do you think that I am rich? I am working hard to feed my family, you morons, you are full of shit, gutless pussies, show your ugly faces, fucking wankers! You pricks! You must be thrown to prison and become some Albanian's bitches! They will make your precious arsehole loose like a cake...'

He moves aggressively towards them and the two faceless destroyers run away! As they go, one of them throws the Molotov into a garbage bin, an explosion follows. And the city of dreadful night is lit again with madness, despair and mania.

My heart is pumping madly. I think I will faint. Dark lights explode within my eyes. I remember the verses: '*The City is of Night; perchance of Death/But Certainly of Night...'*

I start crying. I do not recall how I manage to arrive at Mother' s place. I can't even remember what happened to the taxi driver.

'Where have you been,' she asks. 'Your food is cold by now.'

'Haven't you seen what has happened in Athens?' I ask.

'What?' she asks. 'It was a Turkish film on and was really tragic tonight. There was nothing on the news...'

I am shocked, angry, disturbed. That moaning echoes all around me. I feel that I am going to scream. Later that night the news on the radio announces that six central historical buildings are still on fire. I am more than certain that this will be one of my recurrent nightmares. The city of dreadful night: I lived it. I must go away, away, away. I must listen to *Dido and Aeneas.* Munch, the *Scream.* We are the weak, who experience vanity and nothingness.

Day 14

After witnessing the burning of the cinema, I felt that I had to escape. Something was cut off within me, the umbilical cord with my youth and its memories. Enough with the possessed madmen of this city: let's go, away to the heart of this heartless land. Let's go to our place of birth, to rekindle our horrible love for the Peloponnese, *'the old mother,'* as Nikos Kazantzakis called it.

The early bus, seven in the morning, via Tripolis, all the way through to the Ionian Sea, the shores of our childhood. From then, straight to our village Krestena and finally to the ultimate boon, the fantasy-scape of Olympia. Five days in all.

Despite her age, Mother is frisky and relentless.

'We will go to your auntie, whom you have not seen for years, shame on you, and then to our old house, and finally if we find some time to visit the ruins.'

The bus service, after its privatisation, works perfectly; but we have heard that already. The driver polite and accommodating with a strange sardonic laughter yet without aggression.

'We will take you wherever you want to go,' he says. 'Don't worry.'

Few people in the carriage. A priest, twelve elderly women, a lonely man, and some adolescents with powerful ipods, totally oblivious of everything and everyone. Thirty people in all. It will be a quiet journey. We left precisely as planned: 7.30am. Arrival at destination: 1.30pm.

But whatever starts quiet is doomed to end up badly. Soon the priest, young and well-fed, wearing huge, shiny and air-force style Ray-Ban sunglasses, starts an unexpected sermon against all foreigners in the country. He turns to me:

'You know, my dear sir,' he says with that irritating fake humility of all priests, 'there are so many foreigners that our schools are full of Albanians, Iraqis, Afghanis, Ukrainians and other human refuse from the four corners of the world. They have changed our demography. The next generation,' he stresses his words with his finger pointing upwards, 'will have fewer Greeks than ever before. We are losing our ethnicity, our faith, our motherland.'

I notice that the lonely man at the back is smiling and looking out, at the lovely stretch of land that links Athens to Corinth, through enormous factories, abandoned industries and a soft halo of acid pollution. In brief, he gets angry.

'What do you think, my dear sir?' the priest insists.

Mother replies before me:

'They are human beings too, you know, and we must look after them since they are here. I have read it in the Gospel.'

I feel proud for her unambiguous response.

'They are not Christian, my dear lady (*that fake gentle humility of priests again)*, most of them are Muslims, who had occupied our lands for four hundred years and now they are back to conquer it in another way!' he replies.

'But they are refugees, without any power, how can they conquer our land?' she says. 'On the other hand, it is the help you offer to those in need that matters, as Jesus said.'

Go girl! Play him rough on his own turf.

'If we have brains like yours, we will lose our Greekness,' the priest replies exasperated.

Then, she gives him her personal *coup de grâce*: 'No, we won't lose anything.' She responds raising her finger and her voice, 'As long as we are good and fair. We will lose our self only if we are unjust.'

I feel like crying, out of anthropological bliss – I didn't know she had read Greek tragedies or Hegel. Mothers nurture secretly so many philosophical views.

The priest falls into an uneasy situation. He is fidgety, moves constantly, looks around for support, no support, he settles down, but not really, finds a newspaper, he cannot concentrate, discovers some peanuts in his pockets and by eating them he switches into the silent mode. During this time, he keeps his huge, shiny, air-force style Ray-Ban sunglasses on. We never get to see his eyes. Soon a soft snoring is heard; in the beginning we all think as ecclesiastical chanting in his desperate attempt to exorcise the evil spirits of justice, humanity and love. Soon we realise that he has fallen asleep.

I look at her. 'What you said is magnificent, so humane, so Christian...'

'You have lived in foreign countries for far too long,' she replies, 'and you must have forgotten the true emotions of the people here.'

With almost prophetic gravitas, she proclaims:

'Evil actions come back to those who committed them.'

She goes on: 'You must have heard from your grandmother our family story with the Italian soldiers.'

'Oh, yes,' I reply. 'How could I forget it?

'Well, let me remind you of what happened. After the fall of Italy around September 1943, all Italian soldiers in Greece, were ordered to surrender themselves and their weapons to the Germans. You know of course what would have happened next.'

'The Germans would have had them all executed, as it did happen in Cephalonia.'

'True. However, though they had arrived uninvited, which imposes a different behaviour, the resistance asked from all of us to hide those who could not go to the mountains with them. Remember Communists fighting against Fascists, both of them against the centre and all together against the Nazis – the usual stuff. We accepted two Italian soldiers and had them for over seven months inside a secret cave under the house. Poor things they had to crawl and stay still all day, but at night we took them out gave them food and washed them.'

'That's a story that has to be told.'

'The Germans were roaming the streets days and days to find them. If we were caught we would have been executed. Why did we do it? Because we thought it was the right thing to do. We didn't think. I don't know what educated people like you call such feelings but we simply did it.'

'And how were they?'

'Young and lost. One of them constantly kissed your grandmother and called her "*Mama mia*" and "*Madonna mia*", and "*signora*" and other words which we remembered for years. He was crying calling out if I understood well "*por la mia mama, mia donna, mio figlio...*" The other was more restrained, very silent and distant. He wanted books but we didn't have any in his language, so we gave him the New Testament. He couldn't read Greek but he loved holding the book in his hands.'

'How was your life with them?'

'Your grandfather was very cautious because, as he said, you know the Italians – when they see young girls, they cannot control themselves ... Twisted mind, that's what your grandfather had. He couldn't trust anyone.'

'How did it end?'

'When the Germans withdrew, in April, if I remember well, they were free to go. They left crying, singing, dancing – *mia patria, mia casa* ... Before leaving they did something nasty however for which your grandmother never forgave them.'

'What?' I ask, although I know the story.

'They went out in the woods and found turtle eggs and, believe or not, frog legs which they cooked for us. When we understood what they have served, your grandmother thought that they tried to poison us...'

'But we separated with laughs and jokes. They were crossing themselves the wrong way however; why?'

'It's a long story, it has something to do with certain trinitarian disputes between Christian Churches.'

I have always maintained a morbid interest for Christianity – I wanted to explain the issue, but some other time.

'Trinitarian?'

'You know, Father, Son and Holy Spirit ... Three in one and one in three...'

She becomes totally uninterested...

'Well, whatever, again, why did you put your life into danger without expecting anything from anyone...'

'This is the way that it should be. Two humans were in need: we helped them. It is simple. We didn't think of danger. We saw two frightened humans away from home – and that was enough. Mind you we were still mourning the death of our only brother, who had died less than a year earlier, as the Germans didn't give us the permission to take him to the hospital in Pyrgos. He melted in front of us – only eight years old. Pain and grief. A family without a boy ... Can't you imagine this? After five births, your grandmother used to say that she had four daughters and one child ... After he died, she had no children, as she was complaining, till the last day of her life.'

Silence. Deep sense of immersion. Around us the olive groves and vineyards of Corinth. The Medieval castle on top of the mountain inflames my literary references. I am about to say something totally stupid; but she comes back with things I never knew:

'The same happened during the Civil War around 1948. One day we were hiding communist fighters, the next day, right-wing soldiers. Your grandfather was arrested by the Communists and was to be executed by the people's tribunal, as the communists called it, because he sheltered "class enemies" who were the children of our neighbour. I don't know how he escaped that. Yet three months later he was thrown into prison by the conservatives because he protected two communists who were children of a friend from a village nearby. Until the trial, he spent twelve months in a deep well somewhere in Patras, used as prison since the Ottomans, with twenty other accused of collaboration with the communists. They threw the food to them through iron bars as if they were wild animals and showered them with water so they won't die of thirst.'

'How did he escape death sentence?'

'They couldn't make a case against him. Everybody from the village came to his defence. The judge acquitted him after two hearings. He walked back home alone, having lost his old ways, totally broken. He never talked politics again. He alienated himself from everybody – even from us. He was sad, silent and distant till the last day of his life.' That I remember very well.

Around us the glorious sun is bathing the green, the blue and the brown earth colours into a unique glow of sharp luminosities; the bus is snaking its way through the newly constructed highway made with funding by the European Union. In some crossroads abandoned bridges, unfinished parallel streets, even unused enormous cranes frame surreal desolate mindscapes. Human forms are passing by as if they are thrown from above like puppets ready for their soulless mechanised life. Green emptiness, blue vastness, stony desolation: so many historical sites left unmarked as contemporary misery devours cultural memory.

We stop just before Tripolis at a big café. Local products, wine, pasta, cheese, bread and sweets were sold at unbelievably low prices. Coffee really horrible; it upsets my stomach. The silent man from the back of the bus comes close.

'Your mother is a real fighter' he says with a heavy foreign accent.

'Oh, yes,' I reply avoiding the very annoying question where are you from. 'She is a revelation to me too.'

'You know,' he continues, 'my children are born here. I came to this country in 1992 from Albania. They have grown up here; they speak better Greek than Albanian. Yet look how we have been treated.'

'What's your name?

'Tatz.'

'Listen, Tatz,' I say. 'No country can be monopolised by such morons. You will find them everywhere. And I am not going to let them take over the nation. If they want a fight they will have it: a society based on injustice is already dead. I hope that you will do the same in Albania, if you ever go back.'

'No,' he says, 'believe or not there are worse places than Greece.'

'What are you doing for living?' I ask.

'In Albania, I used to be a musician, a violinist. Here, a bricklayer or now, with the crisis, anything I can find. Still when I close my eyes I can still remember myself playing Khachaturian's *Violin Concerto,* back in 1983. I was only 20, a musical prodigy, the greatest talent of my generation. Look at me, how and where I ended up...'

His whole world is flowing away in those thick, crystalline, Mediterranean tears.

'Thank you,' he says. 'You make me feel real again.'

We shake hands and go back to the bus.

As we move on, the priest starts again his delirium. I have to tell him off:

'Can you stop it?' I say. 'We want some rest and we have heard your moronic ramblings many times so far...'

He looks at me with disdain and contempt;

'You let surrender Greece to Muslims and aliens ... You traitors!'

'I will not surrender Greece to anyone!' I say in anger. 'Especially to your lot...'

Tense atmosphere. The driver raises the radio volume. The horrible Greek songs again. But they diffuse the tension. Nightmare, to thee I surrender my spirit ... Ten minutes of infernal punishment – if a feather falls down, the bus will explode. Finally, Tripolis. The satanic priest gets off; we all feel better. His huge air-force shiny Ray-Ban sunglasses never left his face. A woman who is sitting just a few seats in the front sighs with relief.

'He must have been touched by a saint...' she says, which in plain Greek means insanity – and this is a very ancient belief.

Finally, we cross onto the other side of the Peloponnese. The fragrant green blue landscape of our childhood emerges. The Ionian Sea can be clearly seen, transparent and endless: a miraculous phantasm. The smell of pines and olive trees, together with salty grains of sand carried by soft gusts of wind, are all fused together in waves of visual excitement, of soft vibrations and radiant forms. A gentle breeze moulds them together. The humble bus is transformed. We are moving, but there is stillness everywhere. We remain still and yet everything around us is flowing. *Paradoxical nature of time, at last, reveal yourself*...

Between Zaharo and Kaifas an endless beach with soft yellow sand, made of breast shaped erotic dunes and arrogant tall phallic pine trees. Some of them burnt to the ground after the fires of 2007. Who is to blame? Who cares, of course ... The road looks infinite – in front of us the long alley entrance to the village, covered by eucalyptus trees which we planted in 1968 still in primary school. The discreet fragrance of Australia brings tears to my eyes – or maybe it is because I still recall all these little children planting trees after a long boring speech about the blight of deforestation back in 1968 ... My brother Nicholas as the leader of the scouts is distributing the small eucalyptus trees which now, when he is not here anymore, have grown huge, immense and full of protectiveness. I can hear now their leaves whispering with his voice ... 'Don't cut your fingers, little brother. You are too small for this. Let me do it.'

He is dead but they are still standing, tall, healthy, indifferent – and speak with his voice.

We are here. Krestena at last; inhabitants 5000. All men in the cafés, all women cleaning graves at the cemetery. Very few young people or adolescents.

'They mostly go to Athens or to other big cities,' my auntie says. 'There is nothing for them here.'

Look around: Lush plentiful fertile land, endless fields, olive groves and vineyards, untouched by human ingenuity. Midday we arrive as the bells are tolling. Somebody must have died or must be getting married – nothing else happens here.

Lunch ready; my auntie Panayota and uncle Theo. Solid voices without echoes. Sharp, penetrating, thrifty. After eating, reality comes back.

'We must go to the cemetery to clean your grandparents' grave.'

I knew that I was going to be in a movie by Pedro Almodóvar.

On the way to the edge of the village, furious words about the priest's wife whose sex-crazed lover killed him in plain daylight.

'Noooooo,' my auntie reveals. 'She was the sex-crazed ... She had been with every man in the area while her husband was getting fatter and fatter ... On the other hand, he is a priest and has to abstain...'

Almodóvar, here we come ... Greece, murky country of libidinal calamities...

Cemetery: wind blowing, birds everywhere, flowers everywhere, women in black scarfs everywhere, wailing, sobbing, crying, sighing, noises without meaning, *ich, ach, oooch* ... lighting candles, incense, leaving food for the dead and the saints. I am mesmerised: pre-Hellenic women, performing rituals they don't understand, saying words whose meaning they ignore, the smell of wine, the carnivorous irrational allure of preverbal chthonian deities.

Suddenly, a cry of grave alarm is heard: 'Women, stop, there is a man amongst us...' They all turn towards me; they look at me with curious, angry, predatory eyes. I feel somehow uneasy.

'Don't worry,' my auntie says, 'He is an emigrant from Australia ... he is visiting us...' 'Ah, from Australia,' one archetypal woman says, 'He must be alright then ... We have so many relatives there ... He is alright ... Let him stay...'

They return to their duties, ignoring me. Mournful songs, obscene jokes, incense, incomprehensible tunes. I move silently out of their way; I understand. Everything is a preparation. Soon a priest appears with an old man holding a shovel. They are exhuming the remains of a deceased man. His wife is here with his daughter. As the bones are taken out one by one from the wet brown earth, they are washed with wine and sprinkled with oil. The priest is reading from his book while looking anxiously around. The ritual is numinous, uncanny, spooky. Silence everywhere despite the immense activity; I can hear only birds fluttering around and human voices from the opposite side of the mountain. As one by one the bones are exhumed, long dirges start, shrill voices, incomprehensible expressions, prehuman howls. What are they saying? I feel spellbound, hypnotised by the grip of a ritual I do not comprehend. When the skull comes out, they explode into a primeval song, clasping their hands, pulling their hair, beating their breasts. The birds from around the place fly away terrified by their voices.

Finally, they place the bones in a little wooden chest and follow the priest leading them out of the cemetery. It is a strange march headed by a man dressed in black, and followed by another man with a shovel and six women in black crying endlessly and raising their hands towards the sky. I long for the lucid air of shadowless rationalism, for a transparent vision of death without rituals or wailings, for death as the celebration of life – but I cannot find this here.

Rush back home, rest, silence, the wind, the rain, the stars whispering again, shadows again but friendly, warm, affectionate. My auntie:

'Mrs Maria's son died yesterday; will you come to his funeral tomorrow?'

'No,' I say.

'You used to like funerals, when you were little.'

'Not anymore,' I say.

'Well, we have another option. A wedding: A local woman Antonia is getting married to an Albanian; he is Christian, so he is alright. What do you think about this?

'No, no,' I say. No more rituals.

She turns to mother in frustration.

'You son has rejected our traditions.'

'Auntie,' I implore, 'can you cook some good lamb in the oven with potatoes?'

'Now you talking like a true Greek,' she says.

'I am sorry,' I reply. 'So many years of Protestant influence have taken their toll on me.'

'Don't worry,' she smiles. 'Everything can be fixed with a good lamb.'

She is really happy. The known world is confirmed and I am to be found somewhere. It is only five o'clock, late afternoon. I must commit more patricides before going to bed. Meanwhile, Mother and auntie have filled the room with white clouds with their smoking. Deep sleep, emotional draining, bodily exhaustion.

'You were snoring all night like a lion,' my uncle says in the morning. 'Are you sure that there is nothing wrong with your lungs?'

Day 15

Whispers, whispers, whispers everywhere. What are they saying? They fly around me all night long: 'You are sleeping in the room where your grandfather died, in pain and yet he never complained, alone and in silence. He died waiting for you – but you never arrived.'

My chest is aching, I am falling into the euphoric abyss of guilt, shame and self-flagellation. And now look, it happens: my grandfather comes in, as he was thirty years before he died. He talks to me about his adventures of the Asia Minor campaign back in 1920.

'We were doomed to lose that war,' he says. 'We were unfair, loathsome, abominable. Every time we entered a village, the soldiers burned houses and assaulted women. I was in the middle of all these sinners, one of them, being counted with them. I felt a horrible needle piercing my brain, my heart was breaking; and after the monsters killed the women, we had to march again towards the east – where to? To the Catastrophe – which was ruthless, monstrous and still lasts to this day.'

'And what were you doing?' I ask him.

'I was praying to be forgiven, to find a way to atone for the crimes we committed. We were doomed to lose the war, we defiled everything...'

I see him again that single day we went together under the huge pine tree. After fifty years, he wants to confess and chose me for his admission of sins.

'We walked through the Salt Desert, Eski Sehir; then it was the battle of Sangarios river. Fighting for ten days, so many dead soldiers around. I slept for two nights in half-dug trenches, surrounded by corpses rotting in the unbearable heat of August. I fought fiercely to save them, I fought harder to survive. After some months of doing nothing, the inevitable disaster was near. We were to be punished. It was the justice of God.'

He is with me in the dark, our last meeting finally now taking place, each of us standing on different shores, separated by the cold rivers of existence and oblivion.

I grew up with his stories:

'The glory in war is the loss of the breath of God in us. It evaporates, it vanishes like steam, *puuuuph* ... And it's gone.'

I remember. He never went to any national celebration as a veteran – even when they offered him lots of money and medals.

'What happened after the last battle?'

'I was sure that I was to be killed. Only twenty of us remained. Soon we were scattered all over the desert, panic and horror ... I was scared, so many corpses around. I tried to bury as many as I could. Then, I heard Turkish soldiers galloping towards us. They will kill me, oh God, forgive me for what I have witnessed, I thought, they will kill me. Then darkness fell and found shelter in a cave. At night, I went down the river washed myself and my khaki clothes believing that I had to meet the creator clean and fresh. But the Turks didn't stop! I started walking in the dark. Some Turkish villagers pointed towards the west. I didn't think. I went the way they showed. I slept in caves and hid whenever I heard voices. I moved only during the night eating whatever I could find. Two or three days later, probably one week, I reached the sea, exhausted, dirty, unshaven. I could see an island in the horizon. I collapsed on the shore, cried for hours, laughed for hours – oh the sea, the sea, I whispered, I will die listening to the sound of the waves...'

He used the Homeric word *floisvos* with so much love ... 'Several hours later I heard a motor breaking the silence of the warm September evening; a boat appeared looking for refugees and soldiers. 'Are you Greek?' they asked. 'Peloponnesian, from the other side, the Ionian Sea. Are you here to rescue me?' They took me where the remains of the Greek army had gathered. After four weeks, we were sent back home, humiliated and happy.'

He is close to me; he breathes heavily.

'Do not forget the letters of my father from New York,' he implores me. 'So much agony so much loneliness and all gone up in smoke.'

Now everything comes back to me: the night he named the constellations, the day he named one hundred plants from his field, the day he killed a snake, another night when he left milk for the snake of the house, another day, when he told me the story of the ancient Olympic games, or when he took me to the huge coffee-house, full of gigantic Venetian mirrors, where Asia Minor war veterans were smoking hashish, murmuring lamentations for the brave lads who were killed and were left unburied:

> *'Look Death, what manly bodies we offer you... Eat them, devour them, they will show no signs of pain...'*

Haunting oriental songs, hashish smoke, reflections on huge mirrors: the mytho-poetics of an enchanted childhood.

I wake up and there is still an eerie presence around the room.

He had died in this same corner, waiting for me, while I was frolicking, in Sydney – infected by the cruel, indignant, malignant disease of youth.

The cheerful voice of my aunt shatters the silence.

'It is seven o'clock. Get up! Coffee is ready.'

The Letters

In an unexpected way I found the letters in my computer. Two documents which grandfather gave me a few years before he died. One of them was written on paper with a name and address printed:

'Louis' Little Restaurant.
749 Nostrand Avenue. Brooklyn, N.Y.'

New York 21 Febru 923

My son Vrasida

I am very happy that you are well after I received both of your letters. I am glad for your health as you mentioned in the first letter; but in the second you said that you didn't receive the money with the other letter I send you back on 15 January. I was really distressed. I send to your mother 3,846 drachmas on 18 December 922. The number of the letter is 675028 the registration for the check 30623 with the National Bank Branch N.Y. Please write to me if you received it and I will ask for information from the post office wherefrom I send it you. Everything is very smooth now. I will send you more money soon; I have got plenty; the only thing I want is to write to me a few words and not rubbish. And don't forget that after you will be dismissed from the army, you will have plenty of money to get involved with the trade.

Nothing more

Many kisses
Your father
S.U.M

—

New York 12 March 931

Dionysia, Vrasida, Anastasia and Jeanne

First of all my best wishes for the newly born girl and I hope soon you will give birth to many sons.

Thank you for writing to me; I don't send you any letters because something always happens, sickness, poverty and so many other discomforts. Since last November I have a problem with my hand from rheumatism and I rub it with some cheap petrol as I can't go to the doctor. I had some money in the bank but they have been lost; I went broke and all doors are closed to me; they don't lend me money.

There is so much poverty and famine in this place; more than anywhere else.

Today I received your letter and I reply immediately but as you know I can't do much with empty hands.

If Vrasidas is unwell take him to Gregory's pharmacy and give him a bit of medication and he will feel better.

I will give an advice for the future; when you reply to me write both of you; because I want to see the ring of Vrasidas and Dionysia. I received the letter from Vrasidas but Dionysia has not written to me yet; but I thought that in their next letter Dionysia will write to me too but I received the next one and nothing in there too.

If I make any money I will deposit 100 dollars for Jeanne in the national bank so when she grows up she will received a lot of money. So sleep sweet Jeanne I am working for your future. But I am alone in this country; I am a grandfather who drinks and leaves nothing behind; last night I was so drunk, completely pissed, worst than a priest's woman in this evil city.

Anastasia, from all those trees I had planted did anyone bloom? If you have the time just tell me what happened, I am really curious or if you can't, write to me some Homeric proverbs.

I am bankrupt as I said; so when I come back and have no money will you give me something to live on? This evil city throws me out...

Nothing else; I had more to tell you but I feel sleepy ...
Give my regards to everyone relatives and friends
Many kisses
Your father
Stavros

CODA: Stavros returns from New York in 1936. He hasn't seen his wife and children since 1904 when he left after they had their first boy – my grandfather. He appears suddenly as they are harvesting grapes. His son is by now thirty-two years old. He has three children of his own. Stavros' wife had started heavy drinking and showed signs of mental instability. The moment of their meeting is Homeric: she is with her grandchildren at the field when Stavros appears. She starts screaming: *'Ghost, ghost...!'* The children are crying and run away. He reassures her: *'It's me, your husband Stavros, from Amerika. I am back.'*

Nobody seems to remember him; his son hasn't even seen him. He shows them photographs, letters and finally his ring. After the recognition takes place, his wife starts swearing.

'You sleazebag, you slimy loser, you dumbass crook – after thirty years you think that we will be waiting for you...'

She is drunk. He is exhausted from the journey and faints.

They don't know what to do with him. They make him a room to live isolated, away in the fields in a small cottage. He lives in there almost abandoned for three years. He teaches the children American words: 'These trousers are called jeans in Amerika! How do we call them? *'Jeanies...'* Mother remembers of the *'jeannies'* many decades later...

He had brought with him many bundles of dollars – probably inflationary and thus worthless. His wife does not know what dollars look like; one day, she uses their paper to light the fire under the big cooking pot. He wakes up. He sees his dollars going up in smoke. He doesn't say a word. He walks slowly towards the huge pine tree, which his own grandfather had planted back in 1860. He lies under its shadow. He starts a long mournful song; some time later, silence; he is dead. Heart attack or stroke. They buried him the next day, together with his clothes and everything he had brought back from his *Amerika.*

Day 16

We are here because we must sell an old building. We talk with a solicitor to evict a strange single mother of six children to six different sperm-donors, who has been using it for over eight years without having paid a single euro. But you cannot evict a single mother! She uses the house for many purposes. I have to pay for her electricity and water!

The peroxide solicitor said: 'One thousand euros and I will take her to court.' That was last year. Nothing: the judges were on strike, she didn't file the right case, she couldn't find the appropriate clerks: 'You must give me more money!' Still nothing nine months later. When in situ, I was told that she was also receiving money from the single mother not to do anything about the case: I love rural corruption! It makes me feel so close to the essence of my origins...

Screaming, yelling and paying more money led to the final solution: an old friend, with a strong legal background decided to buy the building. In less than two days all problems were resolved. The peroxide solicitor vanishes, the single mother vanishes, water supply is restored, electricity is reconnected, all legal problems magically vanish. If you know people, things are done – if you don't, you simply have to bribe them.

'Mother,' I say, 'it seems that the worst is over.' We have descended into the belly of beast so we have to enjoy the horrors and the delights of a unique period of time: we have nothing to do but look around, visit sentimental locations, experience the lethargic and wonderful time of provincial slowness.

My auntie decides to visit some relatives. On the way, we hear a foreign voice calling us: 'Mrs *Panayiotaaaaaá,'* with the stress on the last syllable. I turn around: in the middle of that village of alarming and innocuous rusticity, a black man. Tall, slender, thick lips, enormous. Next to him a lovely local girl, short, curly hair and striking white skin, holding by the hand two kiddies, the obvious outcomes of their intercommunion. I am impressed.

'Mrs *Panayiotaaaaaá,'* the man continues. 'Do not forget our appointment for next week.' An obvious child of the Francophone colonies.

'No, of course not,' auntie says. 'Thank you very much. How are your children? This is my nephew from Australia.'

We shake hands. The woman next to him is Eleni, his wife. He is from Ivory Coast, studied in Thessalonica during the eighties where they met. They married some fifteen years ago and moved to the village.

'Mr Louis,' auntie says, 'You have helped me so much. I am so grateful. May God bless you and your family.'

'God's love helps us all,' he replies. 'God's love and socialism!'

And looks at his wife with immense affection. She reciprocates, they are in love. They move on, holding hands. I cannot control myself.

'Auntie, in the middle of this village, in which all foreigners are maligned, a black man? How do you feel about this?'

She looks at me sternly in astonishment.

'What are you talking about?' She says in disbelief and dismay and adds with her finger pointing at my forehead:

'*Mr Louis is not black: he is our doctor!*'

Silence.

'Oh, I am sorry,' I say. 'Stupid me! I didn't understand ... You are right!'

'And he is excellent – the best man in town unlike those horrible Greeks and Albanians who sit all day long in the cafés doing nothing else but scratching their balls, playing cards and talking about whores. Mr Louis is a real gentleman – and his accent isn't it very sweet?'

I am just asking, I say, because it is strange to see somebody from so far away in this small village.

'Now this is his home' she says frustrated with my narrow-mindedness. 'He has a lovely family and his children are like walking chocolate bars, the opposite of you in their age: you were so white and colourless, as if you were bleached. We could spot you for hundreds of meters away. We thought that there was something wrong with you.'

It all comes back to my mind: my albino whiteness until I was fourteen, the laughs and mockery at school by those olive-skinned, dark-haired, black-eyed locals. I used to paint my face with ink in order to be less conspicuous. The pranks and the bullying, the ridicule and the mockery. Where have they all gone? Mr Louis is a good lesson to my constitutive racism and intolerance. The rest of day is simply a contemplation on the event.

Day 17

Every time I go to Olympia I feel like a vampire. I drink the blood of my childhood. Memories start gushing out, images, faces, huge frescoes with human impermanence on display. It was a strange time and a magical time; tragedy was looming but euphoria was prevailing, storms were gatherings but we experienced a Platonic universe. My grandmother who never went to school gave me a map of the region:

'Here, on this huge boulder, women were standing so they could see their sons competing in the Games. On that side, foreigners were standing, Persians, Bulgarians, Turks, who wanted to watch the Games but they were not allowed in. From the other side, which you cannot see today because of the floods, the gods themselves were watching them too.'

'The gods? Which gods?'

'The first gods!'

'What happened to them?'

'They went up to the north, to the cold countries of Europe, after the real God appeared. But we can still see their palaces today!'

'You mean the temples?'

'Yes, these were their palaces!'

'And who is the real God?'

'Jesus, the son of God!'

'And who was God?'

'The owner of the place!'

I still remember those magisterial lessons in geography, history and theology.

I take a taxi. We pass through lush fields and sad villages. We stop at Makrisia for few minutes. Men at the cafés, playing backgammon and cards. They drink and shout at each other with joy and happiness:

'When I get my handout from the government I will take you to the *bouzoukia,* to have fun!'

'Look at them,' says the driver. 'Greeks, Albanians and Russians all together, killing time, the lazy bastards! And the fields are abandoned, unploughed and untilled. It is sad. How can we live relying on government handouts?'

'Well, that explains the collapse we experience today.'

'The European Union,' he says, 'is to blame. It destroyed our industry in the eighties, and later our agriculture. It reduced us to real beggars.'

He breaths deeply.

'Look at the land,' he goes on. 'It has become a wild jungle without human hands. In the nineties the Albanians did everything for nothing. But then they were corrupted by the lazy Greeks and fell into the search for easy money. Mafia, prostitutes, drugs – not all of them of course. But in collusion with us, and with the police.'

'And what happened afterwards?'

'Others arrived: Russians, Iraqis, Africans. The same thing: work in the beginning and then laziness, wasting their money in gambling and whoring.'

We are almost there but the moralist driver has more to tell.

Suddenly we enter into an apocalyptic landscape, burnt trees, ashes, charcoal blackness everywhere.

'Look at the results of the fires in 2007! Sixty people burnt alive because the urban fire-squad and the local police could not coordinate themselves.'

As we approach the archaeological site, all greenness vanishes.

'Do you know, my dear sir, what they did in order to hide such disgrace at the ceremony of the flame for the Beijing Olympics? No, you don't! But I do, because we were here and we witnessed the event: they sprayed, no, they showered, no, no, no, they flooded all surrounding hills with a deep green powder in order to cover the lunar landscape. The television stations were happy, the photographers were happy, the Chinese were happy, they were all happy – only birds, small animals, and even dogs were poisoned by the substance. Did you know that?'

No, I didn't but I expect everything from the Greek Ministry of Culture. As he drives through the frightening place, we remain silent. Just for several seconds.

'Are you from here? You are too polite to be Greek. You haven't interrupted me at all.'

'I was born here. Now, I live in Australia, Sydney.'

'Oh, I remember,' he shakes his head, 'When whole villages were immigrating to Australia in the fifties. Before leaving we had a big farewell festival with dances, lamb on the spit and food for everybody. They thought that there was a dollar-tree, as they called it, you could easily harvest money from.'

'Well, no such tree in Australia. People worked hard, very hard. But they succeeded in the end.'

'I wish I could leave this country,' he says. 'It's poisoning my mind. I don't go to cafés any more, I don't go to church, I abandoned my political party, I don't watch television. I play some old Greek movies from the fifties and sixties or listen to some good old songs. They keep me sane.'

We arrive at the Old Museum.

'Leave me here. I will walk further to the new one.'

'I will be around the corner, when you decide to go back. Only foreigners with money use taxis these days.'

I am alone now in the town of my early childhood. Tourists around, restaurants, cars, tractors, big limousines, buses, the industry of Greco-kitsch everywhere, plastic statues of Hermes, marble statuettes of Zeus, of Hercules, together with little dolls of Greek soldiers in their mini kilts. I have no intention of going to the Museum but my eye catches a glimpse of a big clay jar in its courtyard.

Revelation: my grandmother's oil jar! She kept it at home (*'from my great-grandmother's dowry,'* she explained). The jar was always brimming with fresh and fragrant olive oil until it was spotted by an archaeologist. That's how: there was a time when on every table an empty plate was set for the *'Stranger.'* Just before lunch or dinner, grandmother looked out in the street for any unknown person passing by – that Stranger was to be our guest. Whoever that was, local or non-local, tourist or Athenian, on the designated plate there was food for them. On one fatal occasion, the woman who passed by happened to be an archaeologist. She sat down, around noon, on a hot August day, ate, drank and had fun, and as she was leaving she noticed the big jar. Of Mycenaean origin, almost three thousand years old, national property – unmoved by the supplications of grandmother, the police came and confiscated it.

'Never invite archaeologists to your home,' grandmother used to say. 'They are plunderers.'

But now here it stands again in front of me, smaller than I remember it, less impressive, unemotional, full of sand, an orphan.

I have a quick look inside the Museum. There is only one guard, a woman, and she moves around bored. She gets out for a cigarette. The exhibits are totally unprotected. I even manage to touch some ancient pottery. I have had enough of the allure of the past and walk out. My feet bring me involuntarily to the playgrounds of our early life, to the banks of Alpheus River, where we used to go for excursions with our primary school. I am now in the open plain, away from all ruins; the river runs softly and sweetly with its murmuring lullaby full of litter, mud and memories.

I see again: I am little, probably five or six, and the colossal fair of the fifteenth of August is in full swing. Thousands of traders, gypsies, dark foreigners, monks, fortune tellers, animal vendors, belly-dancers, folk musicians, carpet sellers, the smell of food all over, the intoxicating stench of unwashed human bodies. All appearances are mixed, aromas and sweats, mud and incense – the Balkan mystique in its suffocating glory. I see again: tall dark horse riders are racing. Hundreds of them compete for a simple carpet. I am transfixed. A tall dark Gypsy with shiny skin and oiled curly hair is the winner. In his enthusiasm, he takes off all his clothes and as the horse is still galloping he stands upright on its back. Then he gently sits on it and together enter the waters of the river. There, a strange dance is enacted between the animal and the man: he rolls over it, around its neck, plunges into the water and comes up on the other side – he is totally naked and the horse whispers back gentle erotic neighing. Around them, on the bank of Alpheus a song erupts in a strange language, probably Slavic or Albanian, with the howling of women, the shouting of men, the clapping of hands, the thumping of feet, a vocal pandemonium.

Some years later, in 1971 I think, the dictatorship abolished the fair, because it didn't give the proper image of Greece to tourists and spoiled the lucid image of pure Hellenism. As I rest by the bank of Alpheus, a huge red car passes by with its loud speakers on. The poor farmer with the luxurious vehicle plays Boney M. to the maximum. The air itself is vibrating almost in my belly and heart with the loud music ... '*By the rivers of Babylon, there we sat down, and we wept when we remembered Zion*...'

The ultimate irony under the circumstances.

I have the strong urge to see the statue of Hermes and the pediments of the temple. But no! Resist archaeophilia! Do not go back to the museum. Hermes and the pediment belong to photographers! Stay tuned to the frequencies of trivial specificities. Yes, that's what I will do.

I walk back to find a taxi. It's the same driver again. But now, he is silent – to a degree. We go through the same village on the way back.

The same voice again from the café:

'When I get my handout from the government, I will take you to the bouzoukia!'

He goes mad:

'Listen to them! Six hours later! They haven't moved at all! Sluggish beasts in a self-induced coma!'

He is really upset. In order to distract him, I point out a hill in the horizon.

'What is that castle up there?' I ask.

He looks at me in disbelief.

'You don't know? Oh, no, you don't! Well, it was made by Goulielmo ... The famous knight, Goulielmo Ville hardouino, the Frank, a brave lad, a warrior. Many full-moons ago...'

'Yes, the one who built the city of Mystras in 1245.'

'And the city of Andravida,' he announces with obvious satisfaction. 'A French name, you know, *Andre-ville.* The village of Andrew, his grandfather. And also the town of Gastouni. Gaston was his brother! At least he left cities behind. My mother told me that he was a great singer and an excellent dancer.'

'How could she know so many centuries later?'

'Her grandmother told her so. You know, women never forget a man if he is a smooth-talker or a good dancer. Many of us today must be his offspring.'

We both laugh. When we arrive in Krestena, I ask:

'How much I owe you?'

'Nothing,' he replies. 'You showed so much respect and patience with me; that's my payment.'

He drives away; he didn't even tell me his name. But I learned something about *Guillaume Villehardouin,* the dancer and the seducer...

I don't have the time to visit the other pillar of my childhood memories – the Temple of Apollo at Bassae. We use to celebrate the ascension of Prophet Elias in front of the ancient temple: as in a dream I still recall the priest reading from his old leather book, words that I could not understand, before the sunrise, as my grandmother and many other women were crossing themselves murmuring spells that as she told me:

'They are not for the ears of men.'

But all is blurred: I remember the sun rising, majestic and enormous, and the women chanting loudly:

'Have mercy upon us, Lord, have mercy!'

I was under the impression that they were actually talking to the sun. But the priest was talking about the son of God, which in my childish mind was one and the same.

It is around seven just after the sunset: Mother and auntie return from their usual haunt, the cemetery. They cleaned the graves, refilled the lamp with oil, left some boiled wheat with sugar, almonds and pomegranate seeds behind *'for the birds and the souls to eat'* and now they are back to look after the quick and the living.

'How was it up there?' I ask.

'We had a great time,' auntie says. 'We met all our friends and gossiped. Your grandparents will feel good that their graves are looked after.'

I want to make some literary allusions here, but, no, no, no!

'Last night together, auntie. Up to the big smoke tomorrow and after a few days back to Australia.'

'Well, I have already prepared the best rooster in the oven for you, potatoes, salads and anything you like.'

Around nine, dinner. They talk constantly about this and that; in between they ask about Australia:

'Good food?' 'Do they like lamb there?' 'Did you meet Mrs Chrysanthe's son, George, in a city called Perth?' 'Why do they waste their money on so many fireworks on the New Year's Eve?' And the usual about *Neighbours* and *Home and Away.* 'So many beautiful people in Australia constantly on the beach: do they ever work?'

Before sleeping, auntie comes close to me. She says: 'Don't get emotional about leaving. Move on. We do not deserve to be remembered.'

I cannot sleep all night; I feel that a big stately rooster is pecking my stomach and is occasionally crowing loudly. Crickets, frogs, owls, bats, dogs and cats, all complete the symphony of incongruous sonorities: thus ended my pilgrimage to the illusion of collective and personal continuity.

Day 18

Early bus at seven in the morning. Back to Athens. Thank all gods, but nothing happens on the way back. There is a young priest amongst us, the most common source of nasty agitation, but he is quiet and reads the Bible, of all books. Now, that's a novelty!

We move through lush plains, olive groves and green mountains. The morning is soft and soothing. I look around, while opening and closing, a book. Unexpectedly, the priest turns to me:

'I can never memorise anything from the Bible,' he says exasperated. 'The text is so complex.'

'Have you tried a translation in modern Greek?' I ask.

'But we have the sacred text of the Septuagint for the Old Testament,' he protests, 'and the original of the New Testament. Why should we revert to translations?'

'Because only experts understand the original,' I say.

'But you don't have to understand them,' he retorts. 'We must simply feel the mystery embodied in them.'

'And if you don't?'

'Well, attend the holy liturgy more often.'

I prefer to remain silent.

The greatest trap for modern Greeks is set by the Greek language itself. Throughout it long duration, the same words have different meanings. However as history has been an ideological battleground of decontextualised abstractions, nobody dares to look back and reconstruct the appropriate meaning of each word. They lump all meanings together as if the same word from Homer means the very same thing to this day. Confusions follow: the reduction of the past to a footnote of the present, the loss of historicity and sense of specificity. Journalists thrive on such confusions.

(I am so sorry about this excursus in semantics.)

In two hours we arrive at the harbour city of Patras. The driver says that we will stop for one hour. Mother says:

'We have time to visit the St Andrew Cathedral. They keep his head in a gold case there.'

How could I forget? In fact I remember it clearly: I am four years old, the anathemas between the Eastern and the Western Churches were lifted, Pope Paul returned the precious holy relic to the Church of Patras, after five hundred years. It was transported to Rome just before the Ottomans conquered the city in 1460. In 1964, it was sent back as a proof of the reconciliation between the churches. For the family, the event is the culmination of a well organised religious tour; first to the nearby island of Zakynthos, to venerate the fully preserved body of St Dionysius

(‘*Only his nose is missing,*’ the priest tell us). Then to the island of Cephalonia, for the body of St Gerasimos (‘*He gets up every night and walks around the island,*’ the monk says. ‘*We have to change his shoes, at least once a year*’). We couldn’t go to Corfu for the body of St Spyridon – although we heard with horror that his left hand was stolen last year; however it was found and stuck back miraculously to the rest of the body. So we took the ferry back to Patras, after our pious pilgrimage to the mummies.

Just as well: thousands of soldiers were in full deployment along the streets of the city leading to the imposing basilica, the King of Greece, the Queen, the Archbishop and hundreds of priests, and of course hundreds of thousands of faithful – amongst them, us. Scenes of astonishing religious frenzy take place as the Catholic bishop hands over the precious head. Women and monks scream and approach to touch the relic. The soldiers push them back. The archbishop raises the head high as a trophy and shouts: ‘*Saint Andrew, you came back home! We have been expecting you for centuries!*’

Then, as they all move towards the big church, cannons shell rambunctiously the air, battleships bellow at the harbour, three jets are flying thunderously over the city. I always associate religious ceremonies with deafening sonic pandemonium. All together enter and place the precious head in a small, cosy and cool chapel. Too many people around, so we decide to go for ice cream instead.

Well, we are here now, after so many decades. The gold case around the severed head shines. The offerings of the faithful shine, everything shines. But why? Well, because of the cleaner: an old lady who is looking after the chapel. She holds a yellow cleaning cloth in one hand and a cleaning spray in the other. *Ajax, powerful, anti-bacterial, eradicates grease and grime.* Your religious duty is to cross yourself, kiss the sacred skull and give some money for the maintenance of the building. Her religious duty is to rush after you, spray and wipe it immediately with the cloth. I am amazed by how fast she moves.

'Don't touch the head of the saint with your hands,' she shouts at some pilgrims. 'They are dirty and you may infect it!'

Mother kisses the miraculous skull; the cleaning lady looks impatient. She sprays it immediately and the imprint of mother's lips is dissolved. I remain ten meters away from the scene.

We go back to the bus. The Corinthian bay next to us in a dazzling display of its cosmological blueness. I think that everything is fine with this world. The bus moves. Suddenly, as we exit the city, we pass through a shanty town with small huts made of carton board, broken wood and plastic. Around them are crawling poorly dressed people, dirty, some wearing plastic bags as shoes. They move like animals, on all fours, hundreds of them, mal nourished, emaciated, with red eyes, looking which direction each vehicle goes, mumbling incomprehensible words. Suddenly one of them starts screaming banging his head against a big truck; blood everywhere. The driver speeds off while the dark body of the lonely man falls on the ground yelling in pain and rage.

'They try to hide under anything,' the driver says, 'in order to get through ferries to Italy.'

It is as if we are passing through a modern version of the Inferno. I cannot describe the feeling of being looked at with hatred, loathing and rage. They want to kill us, dismember us, disembowel us; they want food, shelter, warmth, water, help, sympathy, and we simply go through their multitudes with the comforts of modern technology and the cruelty of middle class who don't want to share their privileges. I turn my eyes towards the brilliance of the blue sea. I can see mermaids and nereids and tritons – and I feel content. Opposite us, the miracle of contemporary technology: the hanging bridge that unites the Peloponnese with the rest of the country. All contra dictions in one picture.

Finally, Corinth. Finally, Elefsis. Thank the gods, Athens.

Oh Piraeus, in you I shall rest.

It's only for several hours; Mother turns the television on.

News: *'A bold theft of immensely important exhibits from the Old Museum at Olympia took place between seven and eight thirty in the morning. There was only one guard for the whole Museum, because of budgetary cuts, who was immobilised by the thieves, tied down and gagged. The two people stole Mycenaean jewels, three hundred coins of the classical period, votive offerings by ancient athletes, vases and two small marble statues amongst others. Their value cannot be estimated. The Ministry has been accused of failing to protect the cultural treasures of the nation.'*

Just imagine that! I was there only yesterday! I could have stolen them myself...

Day 19

Back to the heavy atmosphere of the capital; it is a strange day. First, rainy weather, then the sun is out, then dark clouds everywhere. As I am waiting for a friend, an old fellow student from England who now lives here, I enter the Benaki Museum next to the Parliament. There is an interesting collection of documents about modern Greek history in here, some interesting post-Byzantine icons, and of course the cute memorabilia from the wretched Greek monarchs of the last one hundred and eighty years.

All Greek royals had the distinct propensity for kitsch decors and proletarian exhibitionism. The noble minimalism and luminous linearity of folk architecture never entered their world of asphyxiating baroque pretence. Their lack of proportion undermined the cohesion of the society they were ruling over to an unimaginable degree: their inability to erect any remarkable building or create any acceptable symbol consolidated only empty spaces. On their emptiness the unfulfilled convergences of social classes imposed a sense of the *manque* on the citizens and instituted gratuitous hyperactivity without purpose and destination. There is no vertical dimension in the symbolic universe of a society without the presence of creative achievements. The lack of aesthetics of the political order in the country is their permanent bequest to its culture. Their absolute insensitivity to aesthetics abolished all ethical valuation of social experience.

Let's abandon such ruminations however. These documents are so poor and insignificant, that anyone feels uneasy at the realisation that at the level of political thinking absolutely nothing interesting has been produced in the country. No theory of politics, no reflection on the political experience or on the political leadership itself. It is tragic, and that's the genuine contemporary Greek tragedy: the ability to be happy with an unexamined life. On some historical occasions Greeks became interesting to others only because of their catastrophes. The unexamined life is the trademark of the people who claim Socrates as their intellectual father.

Because of this, the Greek state instituted a public sphere with many events but without history. A nation without history hides its weaknesses and strengths under false pretensions about past glamour and eschatological triumphs. Like some novelistic heroes, Greeks produced evil as their own work of art; and what is evil? The inability to accept yourself as you are, the unreflective surrender to the cult of delusions, idols, masks. So they always see stones, rocks and mountains but never a landscape; trees, trees and more trees but never the thick forest of dark presences which you must enter in order to commit the transcendental crime of parricide emancipating yourself from the sweet tyranny of grand narratives.

As I am sitting at the café, involuntarily, I notice the gruff expression of another notorious Greek politician as he is conversing with two journalists at the next table. The ugliness of the face leaves no doubt as to what they were talking. I go closer. Corruption, embezzlement, misappropriation of funds.

One journalist says:

'You have voted the law that acquits all ministers.'

The other adds:

'You have established an unethical culture of legalised impunity for all politicians.'

There is a strange ironic laughter on their lips.

The crude face pontificates undeterred:

'*Gentlemen, everything legal is ethical.*'

The two journalists are taken aback by the elegant phrase. The rustic face continues: 'As long as an elected government controls legal procedures we can determine the innocence and the culpability of anyone: right and wrong are choices made under specific situations.'

The two journalists, also trained in the games of manipulation, agree:

'It is the democratic right of each elected government to determine such matters.'

They seem very content. The question of ethical choices has been resolved.

The echo of that phrase killed off the rest of my day. Centuries of humanism left the political elite of this country untouched, devastated by the anxiety of the inept bystander, which in the end evolved into cheap and rapacious voyeurism.

When back at Mother's place I try to concentrate; I remember Sophocles, Antigone and her dilemmas. 'They assassinate their own inheritance!' I realise, but that's highly symbolic and there is nobody willing to defend it.

Mrs Felicity:

'Why do you think that we are watching foreign films? Because they give you the illusion of dignity, that our local programs do not. Our programs don't tell stories, they don't have characters, we cannot find ourselves in them. In the end of the day, a Turkish film makes me feel at home in the world.'

I don't remember if I actually met the friend I had an appointment with in the morning.

Day 20

In the streets of Athens, people are running up and down in silent despair, struggling to escape a horrible threat that is about to devour them; traffic lights are blinking, water pipes are broken, cars are on fire, the walls of big buildings are collapsing, the underground roar of an unknown monster can be heard, remote metallic clashes, distant cries, ululations, shrill laments, wailings, screams of eschatological conflagrations. Their eyes are empty, no pupils, as if dark mirrors abolish all markers of personal identity. They move, struggling to escape the city, but they cannot, the city is alive, it is a boa constrictor, a minotaur, a Gorgonic shield, it is a monumental trap, that now is awake and ready to start its duty, its natural predisposition to eat everything alive, everything moving and running; monstrous dogs are chasing them, wolves, primeval beasts, growling bears, mythological unrealities without gravity, shadows and ghosts and transparent illusions. Redness everywhere, the streets are foaming with torrents of blood, foreboding sounds, inchoate whispers, printed pages are burnt and are scattered in the air – and that horrible ancient voice:

'*Prepare your funeral pyres! Stones do not want to be venerated anymore!*'

I wake up sweating: it is five in the morning and that bloody bell for the nearby church has started its agitation again. The voice echoes in my mind – how can we end the stone worship that has embraced this country? Statues, temples and churches – the worship of rocks, of stone and of stonework?

Coffee please, coffee ... It starts raining. I have some appointments which I would like to miss but–

One is at the University. As I arrive the building is occupied by students.

'What is happening, lads?' I ask, using one of my endearing colloquialisms. The response comes from a tall, bearded and middle aged student:

'We are fighting against techno-fascism which undermines our right to study.'

'What is techno-fascism?'

'Academics can vote now through a computer system irrespective of where they are.'

'Isn't it more democratic? All of them will decide about the future.'

'No, because not all academics should vote. Only the ones who are on our side. We fought hard to neutralise the reactionaries and the conservatives who can vote again with this system.'

'Yes, but that's democracy – all have the right to vote.'

'No, that's a bourgeois concept of democracy; but we, the pioneers of social justice and freedom, will fight against it.'

They enter the main room where the computer centre is, switch power off, dragging computers out of their frames, breaking some of them on the floor. Other students don't allow academics to get out. They lock them inside the building. I see my friend on the other side of a window. She makes signs with her hands. Tomorrow, tomorrow. I get that. Tomorrow never comes. From this side, I can see the expensive computers destroyed. Democracy in action. I learned a new term: techno-fascism.

First meeting, off.

Second meeting. Down to Piraeus, Kaminia. Just caught the last metro before the strike begins. Midday, I run down the back streets of the market place. Meeting with George, my maths teacher of so many years ago – my first Socrates. As I turn the corner of a very unassuming street, here it is, in front of me, religious otherness.

Oriental men naked to their waste listen to a man wailing, they start crying too; then they take out whips with blades and chains, they start flagellating their naked bodies, they are bleeding, pieces of skin fall on the street pavement, a white armoured horse appears, then a coffin, then they start beating rhythmically their chest, they are wailing again, they are mourning the Imam Hussein, the grandchild of the Prophet and his family, Muslims from Pakistan. After one hour of wailing and self-punishment, they enter a big warehouse. An imam talks to them and they start their religious feast with food and celebrations. The ritual is appealing but the context, *that* context, I cannot find the appropriate prose to describe it.

Soon the Neo-Nazis with their black squads arrive yelling abuse – and police forces arrive too. But the organisers do not understand what the fuss is about:

'Hussein is a great saint for us, we honour his sacrifice...' they say with innocence in broken Greek.

'You have saints too; we have seen the way you bring out the coffin of Jesus once a year. Don't we have the right to venerate our saints?'

There is another battle looming. I must go, I am content, at last the monoculture collapses.

Second meeting also aborted.

After that religious shock, I am off to the third meeting. Egaleo, a working class area. There lives my old friend and fellow student Michael, a blasphemous hang over from the seventies. I called his old phone number. It hadn't changed, his mother responded. 'He is not well!' she cries. 'He hasn't been well for some time.'

I know, I am with him now, next to his bed. He is a drug addict; stoned, spaced out. The most bewitching mind of my generation, the vessel of vatic election, '*emptied of its poetry.*' Sad and abandoned, with his eighty six year old mother by his side.

'Who will die first,' she tells me, 'is the question.'

'Michael, Michael,' I whisper. 'It's me, me ... I came from the other side of the world to see you...'

He opens his eyes imprisoned by black circles, looks at me, shakes his head, makes a painful smile and turns on the other side. He is elsewhere, consumed and transported, in his beloved books of Carlos Castaneda, a page, a paragraph, a sentence. I don't think he recognises me, he wants to be left alone, the poet of verbal euphoria and revolutionary hope, now hopeless and lifeless and wordless.

His mother, an aristocrat from Alexandria, takes care of him. As I enter, she plays the piano, the strange and dissonant and sinister sounds of Scriabin's *Sonata no. 9,* the demonic *Black Mass,* an elegy to the condemned souls.

'He likes it: it helps him deal with his nightmares,' she whispers.

What happened? When? Her son failed to become an opportunist. He failed to follow his friends, who after the Socialist Party came to power, became highly paid public servants, obedient, wealthy and castrated. He didn't like working for any government, he kept writing poems about the symbolic transformation of the everyday *Satori,* about the energy flowing between things that creates sound and psyche and therefore poetry.

His old friends won great prizes for their bad prose, became popular for their derivative verses and some were elected in the parliament for their pompous vulgarity. He withdrew. No publisher accepted his poems, which in a moment of madness he ceremoniously threw into the fire, mourning over the many souls that would never enter their universe. He experienced the eclipse of his own existence; and descended into the silence of solitary uniqueness. He imprisoned his verbal eruptions in the impenetrable fortifications of his genius.

Turn off your mind, relax and flow downstream...

Drugs, acid dreams, the ultimate trip. First hospital, then rehab, finally the mad house. He didn't stop; from magic mushrooms and LSD to heroin and cocaine, the unbridgeable gap in regimes of perception which he tried to cross without teacher and guidance – a missionless Prometheus.

He will die soon. Death flutters around him; he is only a pale, anaemic, diaphanous skin. Blackness has already conquered his room with its thickness and occlusion.

His mother holds with love the emaciated hand pierced by countless needles, lying purposeless on the bed. Tears in her eyes.

'My only child, my only child...'

I remember his dramatic movements and his transparent long fingers calling Mayakovsky and Khlebnikov out of the dead.

> *'Poets of the Verbal Revolution, arise, do not submit, do not surrender–*
> *the moon was conquered but the struggle for lunarity will never eeeeeend...'*

1979, when we took over the university and organised impromptu happenings. I felt intimidated by his idealism, his energy, his purity. But those days are gone, he decided not to grow old, to keep himself in constant excitability and alertness – and one disappointment led to another, then resentment sank in, then frustration, dismay, regret, self-hatred, self-indulgence, self-erasure.

'Sometimes, he gets up, bangs his head violently against the walls, and screams: "*Open up doors of perception, open up*" and splashes everything with blood,' his mother says. He is sleeping now or maybe not; I can feel the rage and the pain radiating like a numinous aura towards the cosmic energy, the luminous void of *'Tat Tvam Asi'*, his ultimate communion with the carnivorous non-being. His mother becomes uneasy. She clenches my hand in despair:

'Cherish his memory,' she tells me. 'Do not forget the great promise he incarnated and then wasted.'

Her hands are shaking, the beautiful face of an eighty six year old girl shines again.

'Go now,' she adds. 'I must wash him for his physical needs – he wouldn't like to know that they saw him in such a state.'

I kiss her hand and walk slowly out: I just met the Pietà with her son, and it was magnificently sublime and passionate and ferocious, the *mysterium fascinans* in all its force and drama and eloquence.

My mobile rings. Mother of course. What would I like for food tonight: spaghetti Bolognese with mushrooms and red wine.

'You shouldn't be drinking alcohol.'

'No, I shouldn't be drinking alcohol. Let's drink coke then.'

'It is healthier,' says she.

Both mother and son died two months later; first the son and the mother followed. After he was gone, she locked herself in his room, dressed in the clothes she wanted to be buried with – and she died five days later. Her grave was next to his: I visited them three months later. I had to keep my promise and read Rilke's *Duino Elegies* on his grave:

> *In the end, those torn from us early no longer need us...*

I read all ten poems to him – and every movement of the flowers on the tombstone made me feel that it was his reply to the beauty of the verses and to my morbid Mediterranean sentimentalism. It was a windy day, and leaves from dried rose petals were flying like lost souls around the cemetery. Like them, the poet ascended to the invisible democracy of language, dematerialised, eternal. He left behind only '*incidences*', reminiscent of Daniil Kharms' loud, despotic and guttural denunciations of what was, is and will be – unsung elegies to an era of high hopes.

> *'Reader! Think this fable over and it will make you very uncomfortable.'*

Back home. The Bolognese is completely tasteless. I cannot eat it but I must.

The third movie: *It's a Long Road,* by Pandelis Voulgaris. I watch it alone. It is on, at a theatre in central Athens, around eight at night. Few people around, munching popcorn voraciously. I am amazed. I don't know how he did it. I never thought of Voulgaris as a director with the ambition to visualise dark infernal emptiness. But he managed to see through opaque decorative motifs and present the nothingness that dominates the mind, as it is turned inwards onto itself.

When a man loses his soul, what remains is a body that craves for self-oblivion. But how does a man lose his soul? When he ceases to relate. Why does he cease to relate? Out of disempowerment due to sloth and falsehood. The personal intersects with the collective. Voulgaris' film was precisely about that convergence point, between alpha and omega, where living a life without resistances leads to the gradual fading of the psyche, the unbreakable centre of conscious existence.

The film is made of three stories, ostensibly unrelated but climactically structured to an explosive end. The first is about absence, the second about loss and the third about the inner void. The last story is the allegory about this country. An old political activist, made money, got married, had children, became respectable, gained positions, social prestige and power. But his real life happens in the sleazy world of prostitutes, gamblers, 'barking' singers, money launderers, slimy crooks, greedy pimps, encapsulated in a squalid night-club misappropriately named '*Viet-Nam.*' Yet, despite the excess of elemental pleasures, he is not content: all his falsity, insincerity, deceitfulness erupt every time that he involuntarily remembers who he wanted to be. His old self confronts him with the traces of his ideals and dreams. He spends his money on sex and he feels sexually frustrated; he shows off his wealth and he feels poorer and poorer; he parades his success and he feels insecure, frustrated, rejected. The more he gets, the less satisfied he is. The more he amasses, the less he has. He gains recognition and he becomes a nobody. He is a human relic, a black hole, an unfillable emptiness. The word '*Viet-Nam*' hails him and scoffs at him – being his youth and his demise at the same time. He burns the place down as he himself is burnt out.

Ashes everywhere, a sunset, nightfall of being, *Der Untergang des Seins,* yes, the obliteration of the self, return to the pre-conceptual mode of being. Nihilism at last, thank god, we are all nihilists now. The end.

Day 21

We finally manage to meet again with Celèste. At the Acropolis Museum. It will be our farewell before my departure. Day: bright, mild and windy. This is one of the very few places that you can see the monument – if of course the usual crowd of politicians and relatives of politicians do not spoil the serene atmosphere. I am rather early – or maybe she is late.

Pupils from high and primary schools are here. They are moving up and down constantly. They all end up outside talking to each other: African, Asian, European and the in-betweens. Life takes on its polymorphous brilliance again.

On the other side of the pedestrian street, the original ancient theatre of Dionysus. How many times have we had anonymous sex in there when we were young? Cries of corporeal catharsis – still echoing around the ruins, despite the archaeological upgrading. At least we gave life to the ruins. Oh, shameless gods of sin and debauchery, I can still hear your sighs and gasps from the old theatre ... Maybe now some young people are doing the same: bringing back to life all fallen temples...

It is around one. Celèste arrives, mysterious and earthy, like Susan Sontag. She wants to correct my ideas about the eighties. Opposite us, the brother of the previous prime minister of the well-known family mafia: cocksure, loud and lamentable. Surrounded by his acolytes, they ostentatiously talk about Trotskyist revolutions – the delusional alibis of the privileged *haute-bourgeoisie.*

We ignore the xenomorph and move to the other side.

She: 'The real face of this country is ugly and grotesque. This is what became obvious in the eighties.'

I: 'It is the duty of the political order to treat its symptoms and cure its causes.'

She: 'It couldn't happen: the interests were many and the personalities involved untrained.'

I: 'You have the duty then to resign and go home.'

She: 'Who wants to leave power?'

I: 'The honest statesman.'

She: 'Honesty in politics? Such a pre-bourgeois concept.'

I: 'Then do we have to accept a contraction of democracy?'

She: 'We must rechannel democracy outside the existing political process.'

I: 'This will lead to totalitarianism – we must expand democracy, impose mechanisms of control over power, and limits over its field of action.'

She: 'Then you will incapacitate the politician.'

I: 'Are we to be left with Machiavelli?'

She: 'Machiavelli is cute; more than anything else we are left with Hobbes.'

I: 'But this makes social life revert to anti-politics.'

She: 'It is exactly what every state wants its people to be: sectarian tribesmen, so that they will never become citizens.'

I: 'How then can a society exist like that?'

She: 'We need Thucidydean impartiality to describe the experience – and obviously we cannot have it.'

I: 'We cannot create conscious history then.'

She: 'Remember that we don't have a tradition of political thinking in this country. Isolated thinkers, only, and mostly living abroad.'

I: 'True. There is not even a tradition of active dissidence. All those who create some stir in the beginning of their career always are willing to accept a position in the public service which will dull their thinking.'

She: 'Indeed most are willing to surrender.'

I: 'Insecurity?'

She: 'Conformism! The official ideology of all political parties.'

We talk for some time; it's already four, we must both leave. It is always sad to farewell the very few people whose vocabulary you can decode. Slowly we walk out of the Museum: students everywhere, music everywhere, human voices, warm bodies. We follow the paved street around the Acropolis. We are not interested in antiquities. The street takes us down to the open air cinema, Thission. How could we forget? So many summers here, with Huston, Fellini and Cassavetes. Next to the catacombs of the early Christian period.

'I remember that when I tried to be an archaeologist, I ventured full of enthusiasm into the open mouth of the Christian underground. I was attacked by millions of enormous rats – it seems that the spirit of god fed them well for centuries.'

Also, in Thission, the little hotel in which a very peculiar writer from Thessalonica used to stay. When once we asked him about Hellenism, being young and impressionable, he started with his screeching voice to talk about the flight of a little sparrow, from one tree to another, and how tired it must have been since it could not find a solid place to rest; and then he told us the story of the Byzantine emperor who betrayed his country during a civil war some seven hundred years ago, 'Just imagine this – only seven hundred years ago!' he said clapping his hands: 'Less than a split second in the time of eternity!' Later, the traitor became a monk in repentance and wrote his memoirs: 'Full of associations, and word-plays and self-parody, the James Joyce of the fourteenth century – you must discover him.' He gave prominence to sadness and confusion.

'As long as you are yourself,' he said, 'you can face with dignity the fear of decay – which is the real meaning of change.'

Now we are here, in the middle of the endless fall, without thinkers, artists and creators, to invent forms, genres and patterns, which could console and reconcile.

'Oh,' Celèste says, 'you are incorrigible! When did you meet all those people? Didn't you go around enjoying life? I hate models of virtue!'

'I committed all the sins I could commit – I am blessed. I can now reflect on the nature of sin and virtue.'

In front of the Thission station; we must bid farewell.

'Do not come so often to this country,' she advises. 'It has a bad effect on you.'

We kiss good bye.

'We must talk about our fathers, one day,' she says – and we are both in tears.

When later that day, I hear the prime minister of the country saying that '*With the help of god, we will succeed,*' I understand that everything is lost.

Day 22

Political mess and social confusion have given rise to shifty opportunism. It is bizarre, but after so many scandals and so much corruption no one, no one has ever been punished. After some furore in the media, everything is forgotten. Memory is selective; clever people make use of this.

A man from the conservative party talks to me:

'Well, I know that we have created the problem, to be precise we exacerbated it beyond any control; but we are in government now. We will wash ourselves clean. We shall de-legitimise every voice of dissent. We will find ways of distracting attention, direct it towards certain issues which always preoccupy the population.'

He smiles with smugness. Then he goes on:

'Turkey, for example, the name of Macedonia, or the increased criminality of the Albanian immigrants. Let us also not forget the internal front, the anarchist groups, for example, or the ethno-nihilists from within, the ethno-haters from the outside. Or the Europeans, generically, who deny our affinity to the ancients.'

'Impressive. You have planned out everything!'

'Not only us,' he consents emphatically. 'The left parties are doing the same. Since American imperialism is not convincing any more, new slogans emerge: the clandestine conspiracy of Neo-liberalism, the new German economic expansionism, the evils of capitalism, just about anything that can be of some use. And we will cause more scandals – and thus more confusion and an atmosphere of disorientation about what actually goes on.'

'That's an exercise in cynicism. You are deliberately misleading your own citizens.'

'It's not us,' he says with a grin on his face. 'It is the media, the press, the magazines. We don't have to do it. Journalists will do this for us. They know how to deal with dissent – they exoticise the dissidents, inflate them beyond their dimensions and thus neutralise and dissolve their possible effects in one go. Some of them also think that they are autonomous, which makes them more charming and appealing.'

'But don't you think that some do understand and know what is happening.'

'We are absolutely certain about that,' he says and starts laughing, as he lights his cigarette. 'But there is no way for them to express their mind in public and influence other people. As long as we control public debate – let them know everything in the comfort of their couch, let them talk endlessly in the cafés, playing backgammon, let them complain continuously in front of the cameras, let them practice self-oblivion in the mass spectacles of soccer and political rallies. We have established the rules of the game and we remain in control of everything step by step.'

'You have managed to completely dominate the semantics of language, no?'

'Certainly, that's the way to control a society like this one. By establishing the parameters of meaningful conversations.'

'How are you doing it?'

'Well, it is very simple: by insisting on the symptom, the side-effect, the epiphenomenon. By entrusting uneducated journalists to define the language of all influential conversations. By stressing minor errors as if they were monumental failures. Consequently, in the public arena, it is predetermined what can be raised and how it can be addressed.'

'So that's the reason we cannot have "radical" thinking in Greek – because we cannot go to the root of the problem.'

'Precisely – although personally I am not interested in the least in radical or non-radical thinking. We have managed to establish and impose a language without references – a language that distorts all attempts to find the truth, or anything truthful. Ethics and conduct for example are words which can be used only ironically – despite their weight in English or French. In our own language, which has produced them, they can be used only scoffingly and dismissively. We have suspended the valorising function of language; so Greeks feel free to say whatever they like without ever thinking about consequences. And I can assure you: they are very, very happy with their valueless language!'

He coughs to clear his throat: has he said too much? Are there any dilemmas in him? He adds:

'That's why they are so interested in grammar and syntax. In order to be protected from meaning.'

I start feeling uncomfortable. I ask:

'Who then defines standards of civility in the country?'

'Civility? Greeks cannot be civil. Greeks should not become civil. Their state will never allow them to be so. They are Greeks only if they exist in a repressive society; their personal identity is consolidated through repression. They must define themselves through lies.'

He wipes his lips, as he spits all over the place with elation. I am getting upset.

'Why?'

'They must spend their whole life struggling against themselves, so they will remain an amorphous mass, unreflective, un-individuated; not only because they can be controlled more effectively but because they must remain unable to discover or imagine their own reality. Their reality implicates many people in power, the church, the army – and no one amongst them wants to be implicated.'

'How do you achieve this?'

'By fragmenting the world, by presenting it in disconnected pieces, by establishing an education which gives a bit of everything but nothing sufficiently, by instituting a legal system in which a multitude of laws cancel each other, by making the vagueness of past history the ultimate code of contemporary self-definition, by raising issues of belonging but not of being, by creating conditions for a perpetual struggle against each other. I can go on with more strategies – but I would be confused myself by their sophistication and complexity.'

'And what do you achieve?'

'The lack of introspective consciousness and thus the imposition of resistless subordination. We establish a mindset and a framework of action that makes them believe in the values that legitimise and vindicate their own subordination. They become dependent on the state, expect everything from the state and thus become in themselves unable to act, desire and think about alternatives. We have succeeded in abolishing their agency and historical initiative.'

He looks amused with my obvious bewilderment.

'Furthermore, personally,' he continues, 'I think that it is imperative for some political groups, to burn buildings, destroy property, attack the police and enact all the political folk-lore that left-wing parties and their fellow travellers usually commit. Most of them are stuck in the sixties and seventies! While they should be grateful for what we are doing: we are preparing the structures that they will support and legitimise their authority when they come to power. And some of them know it and are ready.'

Now, I am really perturbed and in panic. I cough, my hands are sweating, I cannot find a comfortable position on the leather armchair.

'Who are you? The "we" you use makes me uneasy.'

'Ah,' he smiles. 'Turn your television on and you will see us. Read your paper and you will be reading about us. Are you blind and deaf that you can't see and hear the ever-present reality of our power?'

'You seem to confirm the wildest conspiracy theories.'

'Oh, I love reading about conspiracy theories. You must listen to our metropolitan in Piraeus. His immense stupidity leads him to the heart of the matter. Don't they look like a wonderful cosmic drama, which places the powerless at the centre of the universe? It is so comforting to feel that even in a dark and sinister universe, everything happens for your sake: you are the *axis mundi.* It is a great consolation to the drabness of everyday existence – is it not?'

He is eloquent, informed and confident; I remember him as crude, rapacious, suburban. What changed him?

'You know,' I dare say, 'I shall write a report on the country. Can I mention some of these statements?'

He stops for a second and goes on.

'By all means! I am more than certain that very few will pay attention anyway; you cannot be crass and vulgar enough – so no Greek will ever believe you. And please don't you mention my name! I will deny everything. But on the other hand, do I have a name?'

Cold, negative eyes, his big hands, covered by scales: I have an enormous reptile in front of me, out of the Mesozoic period, an ichthyosaurus, ravenous and insatiable.

I am shocked, I choke, I will cry, I will scream.

I step out of his office in the centre of Piraeus. We studied together; he became successful, I became an emigrant. This is my generation? The great promise of 1974? The grand hope of the restored Republic? My generation! I sit on a bench opposite the magnificent Piraeus theatre. Well, I must get used to it: this is my generation, the lucky, untried, untested lot – remorseless, petty, evil. Yet we had everything. No persecutions, no exile, no poverty. So we became criminally dangerous unable to transcend our insignificance – the Demons of Athens.

A woman dressed in black comes close, gives me a small paper icon of St Pandeleimon, and says:

'Repent and Jesus will forgive you!'

I get really angry.

'What have I done wrong to repent?'

'Your impure thoughts,' she carries on. 'Your sinful actions, everything you have committed in deed or in spirit.'

'I don't want to be forgiven,' I say, 'and I choose to be a sinner and I want to be judged on how I act out my sinfulness.'

Why am I saying all this to her? I tear her pretty icon in small pieces.

'You are possessed!' she shouts at me and crosses herself; then she departs in distress, murmuring secret words which I don't want to know.

I shouldn't have done this.

The church of St Nicholas just on the opposite side. Bad memories from that building: my brother was married in there. Having sheltered so much hope and misery, the building stands dispassionate and eternal, while the people who crossed its threshold faded into oblivion.

I try to calm down. I was exposed to pure evil: I have the urge, the physical need, the corporeal desire, to read Dante. I enter a bookshop:

'Do you have the *Divine Comedy?*' I ask.

'I just sold my last copy,' the woman at the shop says. 'Why is everybody reading Dante these days?'

'He captures the spirit of the moment,' I reply.

'I think so too,' she consents. 'I sold twenty copies only last week. Great literature transcends time ... and place!'

Alright, no Dante available. I try to remember some of his verses, about Ulysses, but only scattered words ... *'com' altrui piacque...'* Memory weakens. Decade after decade, I used to remember it all, the twenty sixth canto.

'Why don't you read Plato?' she asks politely. '*Phaedrus* will calm you down and will take you to the endless ocean of beauty. Under such circumstances, you must turn your eyes elsewhere.'

I hate it when booksellers know what they are selling. But I smile and buy the book.

I start walking towards Pasalimani. Gentle breeze, the smell of the sea, the soft movement of boats. Another reality, of innocence and freedom which we lost – us, responsible: what crimes have we left undone? The song on the distant radio:

> *'Old streets that I loved and hated endlessly*
> *walking under the shadows of buildings*
> *irrevocable nights of home-coming, around the dead city*
> *I find my insignificant presence in every corner*
> *lost ghost of my desire empty ghost*
> *help me to confront you sometime*
> *walking forgotten and untameable*

holding a flickering spark in my wet palms
and I was walking in the night without knowing
anyone
and no one no one knew me...'

The pious atmosphere does not last long. As I sit down on the bench along the harbour, I turn around and see at least twenty five people dressed in black approaching. The black shirts and trousers (they are both men and women) are imprinted with the golden shape of a strange meander which closely resembles the twisted cross of the Nazis. One of them comes close and hands me a pamphlet; it reads – all in aggressive capital letters: 'FIGHT TO KEEP GREECE RACIALLY PURE. DEPORT ALL ILLEGAL IMMIGRANTS. DOWN WITH THE PSEUDO-INTELLECTUALS AND THE TRAITORS.'

He stretches his hand on my shoulder and tells me:

'Son of Greece, our motherland is under threat; we must fight back.'

'Listen,' I say aggressively, 'don't you have anything better to do? Why don't you go find yourself a job?'

Tension, real tension.

'The motherland is under threat by you!' I add even more aggressively.

People gather around us. Two police officers on the other side of the street simply walk away slowly. I am surrounded. There will be conflict. But no, no! Calm down, you can get out of this.

A peroxide blond woman, obviously their leader, intervenes:

'Let the traitor go. Patriotism will triumph.'

After some whispering to each other, they leave all together, holding hands, and with the same walk; and as I watch their back, they look like a folk dance group ready to perform. They even have a tune: '*Blood-Honour-Golden Dawn*' which they sing as if they are performing Chinese martial arts in the best Jackie Chan style.

That was my first brush with that mob.

Look at the open horizon. The sea, the sea again and again ... *Thalassa* ... The long vowels, *alpha, alpha, alphaaaa.*

Day 23

Reflections: If Italy has the terrible privilege of having produced the dashing Silvio Berlusconi, Greece has the great advantage of having hundreds and hundreds of little un-dashing Berlusconis, all members of all political par ties, or associated with unions, of both left and right.The small scale of corruption makes their presence so pervasive. You see a new hospital being built. You think: great! They look after public health. No! The important thing is not the building of the hospital, but *where* the hospital is being built. The ruling parties buy votes by mobilising their clients from the specific region, according to internal factions. On many occasions the health centres have perfect equipment but no doctors or nurses. They remain closed – indeed they never work. But the money has been spent and the minister can tick another box in his list of successes.

The little Berlusconis control local centres, in collusion with the unions. Together they create a new avant-garde of self-declared activists who have never worked a single day in their lives and who are rewarded heftily even when they are on strike. Because they are small, they are invisible; yet everybody knows them. Because they are insignificant, they are referred to as the 'underprivileged people,' although very few understand the extent of their power. Because they are so opportunistic, nobody accuses them because they have signed pacts with almost everybody.

That starts from the top and trickles down to the social basis. One of the most amoral demagogues who ruled the country, declared recently: *'The only things I received from my father and grandfather were my name and a watch.'* The name itself of course was an investment bank, a brand like Coca Cola, emanating from the feudal privilege of dimwits to becoming by inheritance owners of cattle stations, living serfs or genuine 'dead souls'.

Unfortunately, he had to govern a whole country which he didn't know anything about, except from the triangle of a privileged kitsch pseudo-aristocracy living in the most vulgar upper class area around the old aristocratic centre of Athens. He had never been in a working class suburb, never visited a factory, or been in a supermarket. He thought that the country was his personal garden and his cabinet ministers were all his personal friends who mostly lived within his estate. Hence they were all affectionately called 'his gardeners'.

Together with them, a throng of subsidized left-wing intellectuals who criticise the ruling families, while being completed funded in their subversive research projects by them. Marxists, post-Marxists, Foucauldians, deconstructionists, ethno-constructivists, revolutionary cheer-leaders are all financed by the state apparatuses they undermine, subvert and wish to overthrow. These privileged revolutionaries present themselves as the enlightened modernisers, the Europeanists, the democrats. No wonder people are so negative now about the European project and have become so disillusioned with democracy. For this reason the rise of Neo-Nazis has become so visible and disturbing. Trust between state and citizen has been severed; the citizen is always confronted as a criminal who must always prove his innocence, a faceless number that must be manipulated, indoctrinated and dominated – in that order.

There exist of course many safety valves: bars, cafés, restaurants and taverns are spaces where history is suspended, where 'groups of friends,' the so-called *parees,* come together, to drink, eat, dance and vent their anger against the system. Such *groupism* has become the official ideology for the state-funded critics of the state. In these havens, the *groupists* fantasise about their alibis and condemn the people who work because they don't enjoy life, by concocting the Hegelian image of a working class without workers.

Their dictatorship of cynicism has totally destroyed any sense of dignity and respect. They are happy because they abolish their conscience. They invent religious havens and monasteries of purity to escape but they end up with more subsidies and more official recognition. And only when they dance, the dreams of their youth come back and devour their mind: only then the ultimate cry of despair comes out of each movement, as the suspension of all mental activity transforms these spaces into dark caves of immaterial delusions.

Yet they feel blessed, without a sense of responsibility but extremely blessed. 'We are a cultural super-power,' they declare in late night television debates while yawning and looking at the watch.

Day 24

Sunday, why don't we go to Piraeus for a walk? No more rustic life. Nobody will be around. Mother is reluctant:

'Why leave home?' she complained. 'Something always happens.'

'No,' I insist. 'Let's go for coffee ... simple and clear...'

It happened that, as we went past the Cathedral of the Holy Trinity, she saw an old friend of hers going up the long stairs into the church. It is eleven o'clock.

'Come in,' she says. 'Don't worry. Chanting will be over in ten minutes.'

'Let's light a candle in the memory of your brother,' she asks.

I love ritual gestures, anyhow. Also, nothing can quench my lust for Byzantine domes. It's also the incense, evoking happy memories of fests and burials.

As we enter, I can't fail to notice the long beak of the huge pelican, who is by now transformed into an enormous stork, as he sits on his lavish throne, august, imperial, stupefying, full of grace. The metropolitan! Not you again ... But it is late. He has spotted me. He hasn't forgotten our old verbal clashes in Melbourne. He stands up. With gusto and mental elevation, he starts preaching against foreigners, half-castes, the Americans, the Germans, the Jews, showering the surroundings with gales of spit, which can be clearly seen as the Byzantine optics of the solar dome illumine the smallest speck of anything under its firmament. His hands up and down: *oooooh,* the immigrants who pollute our race, *oooooh,* the Jews who want to destroy our religion, *oooooh,* those nasty Americans who are envious of our history, plus the Freemasons who want to establish a universal government, and thus, consequently, necessarily and inevitably Greeks will lose their independence!

His stern gaze and his carefully groomed long and bushy beard transform him into a *Tyrannosaurus rex,* ready to devour all pernicious herbivores invading his territory.

The audience stands mesmerised. He feels it. This gives him strength. It sends him high. Ecstatic, in rhetorical rapture, into a god-intoxicated enthusiasm. His frantic rhythm of delivery, his maniacal hand gestures, his weird archaic words (*blah blah blah, the Jews ... blah blah blah, the Americans ... blah blah blah, the Freemasons...)* throw everybody into a feverish expectation as his voice reverberates around, like a murder of crows calling simultaneously from all directions.

'Can we go out? I had enough of this!'

She follows in embarrassment. As we are moving out, his shrill voice is heard: '*Youuuuuu,* I am talking to *youuuuuu*: you who leave the house of God, when God is talking to you...'

We keep walking. He shouts again:

'*Youuuuuu,* I am talking to *youuuuuu,* who disrespect and defile the house of the Lord!'

'Is he talking to us?'

'Let him talk to himself. Don't look back.'

But he persists again and again.

'I am talking to *youuuuuu* ... to *youuuuu,* the advocate of ethnocidal ideas,' the hectoring voice reiterates. 'Listen to the truth and you will find salvation! The Church is here to offer you forgiveness!'

I get angry, furious, nasty. I turn around and with the full strength of my voice, I respond:

'Could you shut up, you fucking wanker!'

Oh, my voice, *waaaanker* ... *malakaaaaa* in Greek, those evocative *alphaaaaas* again, they reverberate around the dome and come back to me as the true word of God ... Silence. Complete silence. Strangely enough, nobody says anything, and as we walk out, we can hear only weak whispers...

Then spake the female Zarathustra:

'Don't pay any attention; *fucklessness* has knocked him on the head!'

Oh mother, I always loved your abstract nouns...

Aloof and without further noise we walk out.

'We escaped!' I sigh in relief.

Don't look back – never forget this.

At the long stairs of the church, groups of beggars and homeless people are stretching their hand out for money. We walk down the stairs. A young priest appears from the right corner of the building. He approaches some of the beggars and tells them in a soft and friendly voice:

'Come down, in thirty minutes ... Free food today ... Bring your friends...'

His eyes are full of tears; he touches them gently with his hands as if asking for forgiveness.

The October sun, always warm, embalmed by the cooling breeze from the sea.

After our adventure in that ecclesiastical horrorland, time for something happier.

Let us go to the meat-market, I want to see an old of friend there!

There he is: Mr. George or at least I think that his name is George. He never told me his name or his surname. I heard others calling him George, so that must be his name. I was researching on Greek cinema: during this collapse no official centre gave any assistance. Despondent, melancholic and sad, I returned to the Piraeus womb, trying to buy some delicious sweets. Between the meat-market and the fish market, there he stood: surrounded by dusty DVDs and prehistoric videotapes, in Buddhist tranquillity, unperturbed by mortal concerns, perennial.

'What are you looking for,' he asks.

'Some old Greek movies,' I reply.

'Which ones?'

'They are old, before the war.'

'Which ones?'

'Well, Gaziadis' *Astero,* Laskos' *Daphnis and Chloe, The Refugee Girl,* the *Song of Separation* and some more.'

'Give me your list and come back in two days.'

In two days, they are all here; good copies, one euro each. I give him a second list with ninety films. In five days seventy are at my disposal.

'Thank you so much,' he says. 'I haven't seen one hundred euros in my shop for the last two years. You give me food for two or three weeks.'

My cultural hero, you give me a whole book.

'You see,' Mother says, 'what personal enthusiasm and love can do! You must always try to find the people who work with the excess of their heart – beware of professionals.'

Mr George is standing in front of us now. He is perturbed and restless.

'What's wrong?' I ask.

'I must close down the shop,' he whispers. 'I can't make a living out of it. So many taxes, extra levies, fines and counter-fines. They are even taxing for the income we will supposedly make next year. All taxes together are more than our income.'

Another horizontal tragedy: the assassination by overtaxation of small businesses. Hundreds of small shops closed. The glory of Piraeus and Athens, the kiosks and corner shops mostly defunct. I can see the desolation of his heart reflected around the city.

'I can probably last till the end of the year but after that, you must find a new supplier.'

I buy another fifty films. Total bill: seventy euros.

'My family budget,' he says slowly counting the money, 'for the next four weeks.'

Crisis has transformed all Athenians into Spartans.

Before leaving, he comes closer and whispers:

'Now that your mother is not listening, do you want any good Greek porn films from the seventies? Tina Spathi, Gousgounis, Kristoff and other raunchy stuff?'

'Thank you,' I reply. 'But I have them all.'

'Gosh...' he replies with a cheeky smile. 'I sensed it that you are a bit of pervert but you know ... What could I say? The customer is always right...'

Day 25

I am here only to rest but no rest in sight. After so many distractions, I will take a book today, a small book, which talks about this place and tries to make sense of it. Martin Heidegger, *Sojourns.* I read it on the plane from Sydney. I am deeply disturbed by its shallowness, particularly by one disturbing phrase. As the philosopher visits Hymettus, he enters the Monastery of Kaisariani and observes:

'The monastery lies hidden deep in a corner of the forest near a spring whose water we tasted. The abandoned cells of the monks resembled a series of caves. The Christian element of the small church still preserves an echo of ancient Greece, the dominion of a spirit that would not succumb to the ecclesiastical-juridical thinking of the Roman Church and its theology. A "pagan" temple was once dedicated to Artemis, at the location of the monastery.'

This is what we should all be afraid of: of not being able to see what is in front of you. *'An echo of ancient Greece?' 'The dominion of the spirit?' 'The essence of Greece?'* Is this real? In the start of his journey he writes: *'The Greece of today could prevent the Greece of antiquity and what was proper to it, from coming to light.'*

I get upset by such buffoons: they create a fantasy, project it upon the real and make everything else vanish. They impose a cult of the dead upon the living. Reality has no beginning, middle or end, no connection, no logic, no cohesion, no stability, no continuity, no unity, no purity, no wholeness, no totality, no essence, no integrity, no certainty – it flows, fuses, mutates, combines, metamorphoses, transubstantiates. Heidegger couldn't see that every human being recreates the human; he thought that it is the *Being* beyond the human that makes beings what they are. Yet every human individual is a different version of humanity: undetermined and irreducible, limited yet not explained by its preconditions. Look around. Each being cannot be defined although it can be demonstrated, it cannot be conceptualised although it can be experienced, it cannot be described although it can be localised. Only the dead are in *the* Being; the living struggle to be in their physicality. We all are frustrated desires seduced by the temptation of innocence.

I decided to visit the place, never been there before, didn't even know where it was. I had no intention of ever visiting a monastery, if not for that short paragraph. There is a painting by Konstaninos Parthenis, presenting its space as a sacred haven full of diffused, transfiguring light. But, as I see it now, the place is dark, humid and closed – not a Byzantine space, which is illumined by the love of colour, the tendency to experiment with illusory spaces, and the cryptic symmetries capturing the divine absence. This is an Ottoman space, closed, wooden, introverted, musty. It avoids openness, it restricts horizons, it defends its interiority. There is no sky in its perspective: it is not relational. It is turned inwards – it never looks outwards. Here the Germans executed hundreds of Greeks just several days before their final departure in 1944. The courtyard in front of the building is serene and asphyxiating. I feel rather agitated and unsettled – probably because of the proximity of death. It is strange, but you can still feel the agony. It gives me the same twitching of heart, the same upset stomach that I had when I walked through Delphi and Jerusalem, or the dread I felt when I entered Dachau and Buchenwald. The inanimate objects, stones, bricks, buildings, pulsate with the psychic energy of so many people who died in this space. They absorbed their vital energy and now send it back. I notice that my hands are shaking – I didn't know that I was such a sentimentalist.

Heidegger couldn't connect with the place. This is a place of murder and annihilation not of any epiphany or theophany. You can still feel the breathing of the people being massacred – the crime still haunts the space, as you enter the dominion of their proud despair, surrounded by the echoes of their last words. Where are these '*flowing architectures*' and '*epiphanies of the spirit?*' The cult of stones, the disguised primitivism of minds thinking in the twentieth century as if they were experiencing religious awe in the caves of Lascaux – the philosophising tourists sipping champagne while talking dispassionately about the tragedies of human existence.

I look at the black monoliths with the names of the people executed and read them. *Agrafiotis Akis, Aivatzidis Giorgos, Alexandratos Andreas* ... The magic of human names overpowers the silence of death – it transforms the great inaudibility into a polyphonic invitation.

But still this inchoate modern country can provide an answer. It has already given its answer and doesn't have to borrow its schemata of thinking from experiences incommensurable to its very existence. It doesn't have to be the melancholy of broken statues, in the vein of high modernism. It doesn't have to celebrate the colourful extravaganza of the Aegean and its aphrodisiac seduction. It doesn't even have to dance its excess of euphoria and sensibility. It can give an unaffected testimony which can be inferred by the intensity of lived time, the immediacy of being close to the numinous, the visibility of the unseen forces that converge into the multiplicity of perceivable forms. It has to discover presence – its presence.

Yannis Ritsos, a poet whose best work, unfortunately, remained unknown because of his political imprisonment by the Left, wrote a strange poem after the death of his first child. It can also be read as his answer to the fact that Greece was transformed into a phantom country, submerged under the idolism of preconceptions and the reveries of specular desires.

What one must search for when in Greece is the symbiosis of presence and absence, the constant presence of death at the heart of beauty and the acute awareness of vulnerability when enraptured by the intoxication of life.

I attempt a very modest and uninspired translation. The poem:

The Pattern of Absence

What vanished, grows roots in here, at the same place, sad, unvoiced
Like a big jar at home, sold in times of hardship
And at the room's corner, where it was once standing,
The void remains crystalised in the same shape of the jar, irremovable,
Shining transparently under the glare, when windows are occasionally opened
While in the same jar which has exchanged its substance
With a substance selfsame and equivalent to the crystal of emptiness
There still remains the very same hollowness, only slightly more
Painful.
Behind the jar the colour of the wall can be seen
Darker, deeper and more chimerical
As if the jar's shadow remained sketched over a sarcophagus

And oft-times at night on a silent hour
Or at daytime amidst conversations
You hear within you a certain sound, sharp, bitter, multifarious
As if an invisible finger tapped
On that absent, fragile, crystalline vessel.

The commentary: Look at what is gone as if it were present – it stands here now in front of us, in the indivisibility of lived experience, ready to be reconstructed, prone to its own visualisation. The ancient ruins are synecdoches of completeness: a hand becomes a complete body, a body searches for its context, the context stands out for its creator. No achievement is irreversible, no triumph irrevocable. From complexities, you deduce simplicities, from tranquilising order you infer the seductive destructiveness of chaos – completeness is given only through antinomies. You achieve truth and in the next moment you worship a lie; you triumph and in a second you are obliterated by unforseen enemies. You glorify what is present and in no time you sink into the allure of dead idols. The dream of all people is to become aware of their evanescence – to understand the insignificance of their own uniqueness and the significance of other people's banality.

Ritsos continues with a second poem:

Absence thus lives its own life, with us or maybe alone

It gesticulates imperceptibly, it remains silent, decays, ages,
Like a true presence with the silent smile that wrinkles slowly
The mouth and the eyes, counted by our own time,
Fading colours, multiplying its shadows –
It lives and grows old with us and is lost with us, and survives in what we leave behind.

And we must be careful in all our movements and thoughts and words
Because for whatever happens, for what is missing
We alone, now, bear the unmitigated responsibility.

Commentary: Responsibility, the terrible word. We owe ourselves to the living in order to pay back our debts to the dead. Our consciousness becomes our enemy and we choose to inhabit the fake world of ideotypes. Instead of looking for what we are and do, we are fascinated by the unreality of how we should be. The present becomes a recollection and the future a frustrating expectation. Existence in brackets – the parenthetical being expecting its life to happen sometime when it itself is not going be around. Something is lost – yes, the liberating force of tragedy. Only when the tragic is revived, the truth of being will be actualised.

For now, we remain content with the lyricism of old photographs.

I am bewildered by these thoughts, I leave the monastery and Heidegger and all such useless ruminations. Reality knocks me down when I return home and commit a dreadful crime. I turn the television on – and there he is – inevitable and ubiquitous. Mikis Theodorakis, the composer. Ripe, eighty five years old, with the force of an unnatural phenomenon, in the middle of the crisis decided to help the country overcome its demons by establishing a political movement, *The Spark.*

He is reading from its manifesto. A long document of words and more words culminating in a Darwinian interpretation of history as a jungle, glorifying every conspiracy theory and promoting an exceptionalist perception about Greece as a 'brothreless' and 'lonely' nation which everybody wants to destroy ... Emphatically, he demands for a 'Hellenocentric' education which will foster pride in the national values. He denounces Henry Kissinger for his dual plan to destroy Cyprus first and then Greek culture. He concludes:

'We must expel the foreign locust from our Motherland, we must rebaptise words like Independence, Freedom, Democracy, Equality, Justice ... The foreigners and their agents have contaminated our words truth, sincerity, respect ... etc ... etc ... It ends with the monumental tautology in capital letters, which I can see flashing on the screen: 'GREECE BELONGS TO GREECE AND ONLY TO GREECE!'

I change the channel and happily indulge myself with inane commercials. Sometimes, you feel that it is the only way to maintain your sanity.

The delusions of Theodorakis show that mythological thinking pervades public discourse. Maybe this is the result of the particular form of Christianity that prevailed in the East: no fall into history, no terror and trembling, only the prelapsarian bliss, face to face with god, or with the post-resurrected body of Jesus, and its phosphoric whiteness, without blemish or shadows or stain. Everything which destroys the plenitude is demonic and sinister: history is a dark abyss, it never happened, it never took place. Our innocence shows that we are still in paradise: we never left, we never tasted knowledge, we remained faithful to the original covenant. Everything that happens is wrong but we cannot be blamed for it: it is the others who are responsible – but we cannot be *othered,* because we have remained faithful.

But there is more mythology in actual life: mother gives me a small piece of paper. It advertises the services of the: '*Very Great Psychic Batura*' promising '*Results in Seven days.*' '*Prof. Batura,*' it proclaims: '*international African Spiritual Healer and Advisor.*' The English text, like the Greek, is magnificent:

'Over 20 years experience no matter what your problems are I can help you solve the most difficult once in the fastest way that any one does when you have been disappointed by other spiritualists. I can

bring the loved once more than they are before. I can bring unknown one in love. I also give powerful talisman for protection. Impotency sexual court case exams carrier. Successful business depression and many other things.'

'Mrs Felicity visited Professor Batura yesterday!'

'What for?'

'For the powerful talisman he promises.'

'Did she get it?'

'Oh, yes, after paying hundred euros.'

'What is this talisman?'

'Well, it was the bone of a rat wrapped with the tiger's skin.'

'What sort of rat is that?'

'Imported from Africa. She had to eat some of its flesh too.'

I have had enough, I will throw up any minute...

'Now, she has to wait seven days for the results...'

No more, please no more...

In ten minutes Mrs Felicity emerges: around her neck, the talisman. She describes the ritual she went through, sprinkled with blood of a goat and the urine of an ox; how she smoked some kind of pipe and how she ate the rat. She tells me that there were many people there too, at least ten, and that Batura the psychic knew everything about their previous life. He touched her breasts and squeezed her nipples; with two men that they were at the meeting he inserted his staff in their bottom.

'Where are such things happening?'

'At the centre of Athens,' she says enthusiastically. 'Batura told me that if they don't have genuine rats from Africa, the best they can find are from around Omonoia Square. For a certain reason, rat's flesh is more effective if it comes from the centre of Athens.'

I will throw up – it is inevitable.

Day 26

I thought that it would be a quiet day, a day of reflection and meditation. Too many surprises had waited for me in this country. Just some rest. Let me go to Athens, to that quiet bookshop just close to Omonoia square. Let me reflect on lost identities that I cannot reconstruct and on dark habits that cannot be elucidated. In short, today I am despondent and pessimistic. Take me to a bookshop, I say to myself; you don't have to buy anything – just inhale the smell of the printed paper, the ink, the glue on the spines, the rustle of compressed pages, the mustiness of confined spaces – the dazzling artfulness of Greek books. I am in there right now. I open books and close them; I start the first line and go immediately to the last; I touch their cover and immediately feel the authorial presence, the anxious call of felt temporality for reciprocity.

But human voices come in, encircle me and take over the place. Furious voices. I manage to hear something of oriental chanting.

As I step out, I see them. Having taken over the square itself, a gathering of at least one thousand Muslims, screaming and shouting against the defilement of the Holy Book by a policeman and the screening of an American film on the life of the Prophet. I make the mistake of crossing the street to see closely and suddenly I realise that I am surrounded by the police on one side and the fanatics on the other. How will I escape now? I take cover behind a car, together with some other people who happened to be passing by.

Meanwhile, the Muslim soldiers are shouting in their language, soon they attack the police force, more police appear, more Muslims arrive, tear gas from one side, stones and bottles from the other, we, in the middle, unable to move, tears in our eyes because of a film we haven't seen.

Next to me there is an elderly lady, who cannot breathe. Three more people are huddling with us behind the car. I take her hand and shout to the police:

'Can you help us? There is an elderly woman here!'

One police officer replies: 'Stay where you are. It is dangerous. We will get you out soon!'

We are waiting but nothing. An uneasy silence prevails. We become edgy; one of the trapped citizens cries and mumbles something about his mother. Stones and bricks are flying over us. As we stand still, the elderly woman starts talking to herself, gasping and mumbling incomprehensible words and singing broken arias. *Mori, mori, mori* ... Fancy that: signing *Tosca* amidst such chaos! I try to calm her down – and it is then when the unbelievable happens.

The elderly lady, she must be eighty I think, jumps up like a spiral and starts abusing everybody with the vilest language I have ever ever heard. First she turns her posteriors to the police, lifting up her skirt:

'Lick my arse, you jerks! Smell my saggy pussy, you faggots! I haven't washed it for days. No money for soap ... Can I use your tongue?'

The police are stunned; some laugh, some turn their faces away, some play awkwardly with their weapons.

Then, undeterred, she turns to the warriors of Allah. She squeezes her breasts to make them look firm again and shouts:

'You know how many cocks have splashed their spunk on my titties? Big cocks, small cocks, fat cocks. *A l'espagnol ...* I bet you never dared to do that to your wife's nipples.'

The soldiers of Islam are astonished and look at each other in utter bewilderment. Both the police and the warriors stand still not knowing what to do – for a minute or two, as long as the swearing lasts, there prevails an eerie stillness and immobility. It reminds me of the 'Stop Exercise' in the Gurdjieff movements.

The woman continues to swear in the obscenest imaginable manner; something about her deep-throating skills, something more about licking testicles, something extra about sex toys – it is magic! They are all confused and so I manage to run away.

I look back: green flags everywhere, big placards with sayings in Arabic from the Koran, burning cars, broken windows and destroyed shop fronts. But amidst them the archetypal feminine rules supreme and the armies of men lower their weapons saluting her presence. The woman walks slowly and ceremoniously away. Her last words of wisdom I could hear are:

'You all need a donkey's dick up your arse ... Only then you will understand how sweet life is...'

As she turns the corner, the fight starts again.

After the religious strife and the *prima donna,* a meeting with some good friends. They invite me to a horrible place, where the mob of the *nouveau riche* created by the socialist aristocracy hang out and prepare to exchange their boredom for dreams of revolution, and if not, of cocaine and sexual debaucheries.

We are at a luxurious restaurant. We have dinner. The atmosphere is warm and makes everything sincere despite the fiendish surroundings.

My ears however are constantly distracted by two virile men in their early forties at the next table. They use a peculiar language: partly German, partly, Italian, partly French, partly Greek, with thick foreign accents. The one probably Slavic, the other unidentifiable. I cannot help but overhear:

'How many did you do in Sarajevo?'

'Around fifty ... (*inaudible sounds*). Muslims and Christians...'

'Me too ... I was with the Serbs ... but I was bought out by the Muslims (*both laugh loudly*) Money ... Gold ... Dollars...' (*something else equally indecipherable*) .

They are mercenaries, selling death to the highest bidder.

We keep solving the problems of humanity. They carry on:

'Were you in Kosovo too?'

'Yea, with the fucking Serbs again! They didn't pay me well!'

'You should have joined the Albanians! Heaps of money in American banks, women, drugs and wild sex all night. How did I survive?'

'Probably we must have been shooting at each other ... (*both are laughing*) twenty bodies down...'

'Ha, ha, ha ... can you imagine?' (*I cannot hear*)

'Now where to?'

'Well, Kosovo is *kaput ...* Who knows then? Somalia? But mad savages...'

'I am heading to Sierra Leone or Mali. Big guns, cocaine, the best brothels as long as you don't get AIDS...'

'Where is your agent?'

'Here in Athens, a local politician and minister in the government. Call this number. Say that you need medical assistance.'

They keep talking, we keep talking. Two parallel conversations.

I need time to process this.

Day 27

Nothing planned for today. But I must visit Mr Clearhos, the musician. What he said about Gurdjieff stuck in my mind.

'Go now,' Mother says, 'because he is going back to Albania, since there is no work here anymore. He will be leaving tomorrow, by bus.'

I rush to his place; ring the bell. He is alone packing up, the photographs are not on the walls any more, the empty room now shows all its poverty or else geometry.

'After twenty two years', he says, 'going back home. An admission of defeat and humiliation. My compatriots are envious and zealous; they will think that I made lots of money, whereas I never managed to save but several thousand euros. Why did you come?'

I am cruel and stupid; I don't want to know anything about his drama: I only want to know what he knows about Gurdjieff.

He sighs. 'He was interesting, was he not?'

Not the proper word to describe him, I think.

'I was about twenty years old in Saranda, when, on the radio, I heard for the first time his music performed on the piano. I felt immediately synchronised with the relentless flow of silence that was dancing out of its sounds. It was bizarre; but I also understood that the piano was not the instrument for his kind of music.'

'I must admit,' I interrupt, 'I have a soft spot for Keith Jarrett's performance. I had my own moment with it. On the island of Ios, in 1985, as the sun was setting at the horizon, enormous and transformative, somebody was playing on tape the sacred hymns. It was as if time stopped – absolute stillness, complete immobility, yet people were moving, cargo ships were sailing through the horizon, the wind was blowing, the trees were shaken but all stood still at the same time.' My Proustian moment of that summer.

He takes out of its case another instrument, a kind of flute. 'It is the *ney'*, he smiles affectionately, 'the *kiz ney.* Subtle sound for subtle hands and subtle ears. An old Bektashi Dervish taught me secretly to bring it to life during the years of communism. He was a *dedebaba,* if you know anything about this.'

'No, I don't.'

'It's a pity! Intellectuals do not look for initiations anymore and miss the enigma of insignificant people like myself.'

He starts playing a brief piece entitled *'Short Prayer from the Holy Book.'* I remember it vividly. The vibrations of the sound penetrate the walls, make materiality connect with the passions of human existence, warming the heart of the infidels to the lamentations of the weak. Sounds distinct and separate, unromantic, unemotional, unmoving, paradoxically forming a continuous wave of vibrations, as if the energy of objects is suddenly released and the flows that create balance converge and crystallise human presence.

People look through the window. Music gathers bodies around its source, as people remember and reassemble. We are all here, around fifteen people, listen: the music has unearthed their lost centres of balance. He stops with a sigh.

'But why are you leaving Mr Clearhe?' asks a woman from the window. 'Soon the situation will get better here and you will find work again.'

He places the instrument back in its case, gently covering it with velvet cloth.

'Time to go home, Mrs Theodora. I wandered for far too long away from my roots. Time to clean up our grave.'

I hold his hand as he bursts into tears. I understand. He knows it. We are lost in the same Zone.

His two friends arrive. I must go. We shake hands.

'Have a safe journey' I say. 'Maybe you will find more than you expect.'

He remains silent, tears in his eyes, the mysterious and vulnerable sentimentality of the Balkans. He looks around the empty room. The imprints of his photographs are still visible on the walls.

'Don't forget to pay the rent before leaving tomorrow, if you have the money, of course,' says Mrs Theodora.

I couldn't forget the sadness in his eyes. I must leave the most significant details unsaid – ellipsis is all.

I suggest to the ladies to go out for dinner that night. Mother always avoids open spaces. Mrs Felicity has her husband to look after. But the night is poetic and warm, the moon shines like a huge silver coin, the streets are empty.

'Let's go to the restaurant *Istanbul.* Good food from the City!'

Oh yes, the city ... *the* City!

Mrs Felicity: 'When we visited, the Turks were very friendly.'

Mother also remembers her visit back in 1982: 'Great buildings,' she says. 'Who built that big church with the dome? It looks like the Hagia Sophia we have in our neighbourhood.'

'Mum', I dare say, 'Hagia Sophia in *The City* is the model of all Byzantine churches.'

'Yes,' she replies, 'but our Hagia Sophia here is not Byzantine – it is Greek!'

It is complicated, very complicated. It seems that, although she went through the school system, she didn't do the identifications she was asked to do – unless she starts forgetting, as in the early stages of dementia. I must watch that space.

'Ok, whatever, now it is Turkish!' she says. 'Let's go to the restaurant.'

It is up on the small hill, where we used to walk so many nights as children, when she was young and beautiful. Men stopped to look at her in admiration. Now I have to lead her here, carefully, slowly, cautiously. She holds my hand and leans on me; many years ago she was at the same spot, running as fast as she could to stop my brother from falling down. She grabbed him in the air: she was wearing a mustard yellow jacket and skirt, white shirt and was holding a black handbag, which she let fall on the ground. She was slim, reserved and elegant. She used to cry when she was alone and talk to herself waiting for somebody to appear but nobody was listening or ever paid attention and in the end she lost the desire and the ability to communicate. She turned into herself, where she had to face the monsters of her youth and the nightmares of her present, us, the living proofs of her submission. The wind is blowing mildly. After she catches my brother, she says affectionately:

'We all want to fly, I know, but this is not the way.'

Places, memories, flickering moments in the endless flow of lost attachments.

We enter the restaurant. We sit down and here we are: Mr K. again, the one we met at the very second day of our arrival. The opportunist, the chameleon, the successful. Feasting abundantly with his very many friends, with money probably taken as commission by the armaments industry or from some other national investment. It is all writ large over their clothes, manners, language, public persona:

'*We made money and get fucked, all of you!*' Socialism for ever!

Unfortunately we sit almost next to them. We exchange several words of politeness between our teeth. We despise each other. In few months, he will be taken to court and be sent to prison. He will escape punishment but he will be disgraced – rejected by all his many supporters, he will end up with the Neo-Nazis – his metaphysical punishment. In a few months he will be shouting slogans all over Athens '*Greece belongs to the Greeks*' and '*Empty Greece from foreign vermin*' and '*Death to the enemies of the immortal nation.*' Like a whole generation, the only thing he learned was to shout slogans, and reduce everything to slogans. But right now he is enjoying his petty triumph.

We try to order food but their voices are covering everything. '*We shall triumph*', '*The invaders will be kicked out,*' '*We don't need anyone*' and all of them together the most lethal slogan of the unforgettable past: '*Greece belongs to the Greeks.*'

The noise pollution is deafening. I ask if we could move further, finally we do. We can see them panoramically from here. They are singing communist songs of the forties, they are very content and ecstatic, in their ritual of self-infantilisation.

The place looks nostalgically oriental, the moon hovers over us with affection, the sea is a mirror multiplying the lunar mystique. We are in the middle of all that. And reality pulsates with all its generosity and bitterness as our own ritual of farewell takes place unconsciously around a table, mediated by forks, knives and food.

Alright enough, too noisy here, time to go back.

We take a taxi; the driver is a young man with an accent.

Mrs Felicity says almost aggressively:

'Are you Albanian?'

'Born here,' he replies.

'You come here and take our jobs,' she replies scoffingly.

'Mrs Felicity,' I interrupt, 'he was born here, in this city. He is one of you.'

She pauses; she is trying to find a way out, she does not want to confront me.

The young driver talks like a typical Greek of his generation: *seriously, anything goes, whatever, basically, oh perfect, it doesn't exist.* But there is more to him.

'My mother,' he says, 'was killed outside Corinth in a car accident when I was ten. I grew up alone, with my father, who went back to Albania recently but I stayed on. I don't know Albania. I haven't been there. This is the only country I have known since day one of my life.'

The tragedy breaks the ice and opens her heart.

'You have suffered a lot. This country of ours causes much unhappiness. And we know nothing about the problems of our neighbours.'

She is confirming him local now.

'Where do you live?' she asks.

'On Rallis Street up in Egaleo.'

'I worked hard up there during the seventies.'

She is confirming him native now. He is happy.

'If you think again, there is room for all of us in this country.'

Mrs Felicity says looking at him with motherly affection. They are friends now.

It is already midnight and as we step out of the taxi, as if in a strange vision, we see a woman dressed in black, holding two enormous black dogs by the leash.

We jumped back into the taxi, as the dark trinity passes by silently and solemnly.

'Jesus Christ' says Mother. 'What are they?'

'Mother of god,' Mrs Felicity crosses herself. 'They look like demons.'

'Great be the name of Allah!' says the driver. 'They do look like demons.'

'Keep your gods away,' I reply. 'She is like Madonna in her video clip *Frozen,* if you have seen it. Like the Celtic witch, Morgana...'

The dark lady with the black dogs turns back and looks at us and then turns around the corner and vanishes.

To this day, I have been unable to discover her identity.

Day 28

It is one of my last days. Consequently, all had to finish with a big bang. Around ten in the morning, we go to the open market where independent producers sell anything at half price. Mother and I, pushing our way through hundreds of vendors and customers, connecting with the complex mosaic of the city, become part of the common movement in places where old cultures meet and new cultures emerge. It is exhilarating: the body odours of so many different people, the different hand gestures, the peculiar facial expressions, the anxiety of the poor, the agony of the poorer.

Mother approaches a woman and her little boy, probably from Pakistan, selling some shabby vegetables.

'We must buy from them,' she says. 'They live close by and I usually give chocolates to the boy.' I cannot resist good deeds.

As we are giving them two euros for some vegetables, an enormous body with the smallest head imaginable comes between Mother and the woman. He starts pushing her back, shouting close to her face:

'Don't buy anything from foreigners. They destroy local business. They are not Greek. You must show patriotism.'

She replies valiantly: 'And who are you to tell me how to spend my money?'

'We are the true patriots,' the small head shouts. 'We love our country!' And giving the Nazi salute, he shouts: '*Blood – Honour – Golden Dawn!*'

I intervene: 'Do we hate this country? Why do you want to monopolise patriotism?'

'Because,' he shouts, 'we are the pure blood of Greece and we will protect it from every contamination!'

I push him back, he pushes me back, again and again, and then I do it: I punch him with so much strength, which I didn't know I possess. He falls on the ground. I haven't used my fists since I was fifteen. I am thrilled, amazed, elated – but no, not afraid! My hand is in a terrible pain. I approach him. I am afraid that I killed him. Going to prison for killing a Nazi ... That's a good story for a novel!

'Are you ok?' I ask stooping over him.

Most people support me and start shouting:

'Go back to your cage! You apes, filthy Nazis!'

I am happy, they are doing their civil duty, I am really happy. But others get aggressive. Their battle-cry is heard again: '*Blood – Honour – Golden Dawn.*' Ready for a fight: '*Oh time, where is your dominion!*'

As I look over him, I hear inarticulate howls and two more or maybe three small-headed muscular apes appear over me. One grabs my hands from behind and the other starts beating me on the face and the stomach. The one fallen on the ground, gets up and starts yelling at me very close to my face: he hasn't brushed his teeth and stinks of garlic.

'You want to be smart ... You arty farty fuckwit!'

A cacophony of punches begins, swearing and more swearing. Mother is screaming, people from around are shouting ... Oh happiness, I whisper to myself, oh yes ... The ultimate happiness of every masochistic democrat abides in such events! Unforgettable. My blood for democracy, open society and free speech ... Oh yes, *We shall never surrender* ... *I have a dream* ... *The tide is high.* .. I am passing *ouuuut*...

By the end of the brawl, one tooth less, bruises on my face, swollen black eyes, mobile phone destroyed and some parts of my body numb and senseless, blood all over my clothes. Nothing serious, just messy; and let's see if my new white shirt could be cleaned from the blood.

Mother is still yelling:

'Beasts, the communists were right when they were slitting your throats with rusting tins during the Civil War!'

'Mum,' I groan. 'Restrain yourself!' As I cross the gate towards the black territory of senselessness – yet I cannot stop laughing.

I wake up in a lovely Greek hospital. No nurse for five hours, doctors up and down, looking awry, nurses busy smoking; when we ask for water, they discreetly demand five euros:

'Or else buy your own bottles from the supermarket.'

'Don't give them anything,' I shout, 'Let's go back home.'

We jump in a taxi:

'Don't worry, I feel fine, only one tooth lost. We will fix it.'

There was no reason to report this to the police – I know.

Not even a god can save us now...

Day 29

In bed, recovering from the Nazi imbroglio. A dentist from next door cauterised my empty gum. Not in pain anymore; but still that gap! Some bruises on the face. Later that morning, I went to a private doctor:

'Thank god,' he says, 'you have some extra fat around your belly and it protected you from any serious damage to your vital organs.'

You see: I knew that I was doing the right thing when I was devouring those chocolates, lambs and mousakas...

On Sunday, departure. Finally, at last, I have had enough, I cannot wait: if I stay longer, I will end up in a concentration camp.

My friend of days past, Vasso, called in after noon. She met Mother in the super market who re-enacted for her my distressing yet admirable exploits, adding of course certain important extra details to give the incident its appropriate architectural style.

We hadn't met for long; although we worked so closely for over fifteen years in her magazine. Vasso, Hercules and myself, the young Elias also who left before witnessing our demise. We had the crazy idea of reconfiguring perceptions about the Greek experience, or about experiencing in general.

Unintentionally, we came up with some common principles:

'Be contemporary, discover nowness, ignore the allure of symbols.'

Hercules wanted to grapple with the immediate and the unmediated.

'I like your writings,' he told me in the beginning of our friendship in 1988. 'Your readers never understand where you are leading them – maybe because you yourself do not really know or care.'

He recommended: 'No silly preoccupations with identity, no stupid anxiety about belonging.'

'So what is to be written?'

'Lived reality can never be conceptualised; reality misleads – it is polymorphous, disjointed and diffused. My advice: '*Describe your shortcomings. Insist on the dynamic discontinuities that have shaped this society. Human presence is understood only as a series of breaks and silences. Our great privilege may perhaps be to sense the forthcoming breakdown within our own self-perception, before it happens. Our catastrophe is our self-realisation.*' He was extremely didactic, at times.

Vasso insisted on the quivering of the body, the trembling of the human voice, the fragility of having a body that feels helpless and asks for redemption. She wanted to transform the frightening ugliness of

Athens into the pulsating energy of a private secret. For her, all writing explored the tendency of the human mind to succumb to its own illusions.

Hercules: *'Do not judge, do not fragment, do not ambiguate.'*

Vasso: *'The text you wrote about Cavafy is in reality about Kazantzakis. Are you sure that you can distinguish between them?'*

Hercules: *'Euphony; Eurhythmy; Eutaxy.'*

Vasso: *'Your neologisms alienate readers from the argument. Can you restrain yourself to only one new word per text?'*

Hercules: *'Long, unbalanced, soulless: you become very academic, don't you?'*

Vasso: *'Your essay is a magnificent delirium.'*

She comes in with the mood for an apologetic reckoning. We have many shadows to bring back to gravity, first amongst them, Hercules. He died in 2003 unexpectedly. She enters silently, starts smoking immediately and with her deep voice chides me:

'Feel happy. I left my cats for you. We have no time. Let us sum up.'

'There are no symbols to stand for the contemporary experience in this land,' I begin.

'The only symbols that can exist are the names of our friends,' she replies.

'Two hundred years of independent life without politics. History has become our own specific strategy for ignoring the present. History is our religion.'

'It happens with many nations,' she states. 'Societies that cannot cope with ambiguities succumb to the allure of origins.'

'Aren't we different in any way?'

'Your ideas are symptoms of utopian expectations about this country.'

'I know. It's my diasporic idealisations. But to me it is so obvious, as I come from outside: our people are Greeks but they also pretend to be Greeks – they have concocted a role around their own identity.'

'That's our modern tragedy. We have substituted culture with self-dramatisation.'

'All my life I fought against this representation of the country as a picturesque and exotic toy-land. Like the great Aegean deception, the islands, the sloth of blue delusions.'

'You moralise.'

'I want to find out what keeps their inhabitants alive – not see them through Polaroid.'

'Well, tragedy begins in us, with the tendency to obscure the reality of others.'

'But that's what I find here: melancholic faces abolishing reality by their unwillingness to act.'

'That's a problem not only confined to the Aegean islands and their inhabitants.'

'Certainly, but there I discovered the disastrous all-consuming monsters of tradition, the eclipse of any ethical resistance. Our language is the abode of *lethe* and not of *aletheia.*'

'You are tired and frustrated: language makes a path through the dark forest of others. Language annuls, which means there is no meaning in it. We attribute the meaning – if we have any meaning to attribute.'

'What about the history of language?'

'Oh no, linguistic history again ... You are really unwell! What makes you think that Greeks own the Greek language? My cats are more interesting than you. I will come back tomorrow.'

She is still around, *la donna velata,* so material in her absolute alterity. She sees my book next to the bed.

'Still reading *The Life and Adventures of Alexis Zorbas!'* She derides me. 'I thought that your early enthusiasms were over years ago.'

I retaliate defensively: 'Kazantzakis' language makes this world habitable.'

'It has caused so much confusion, that Zorba of his.'

'It has been misunderstood, that's why.'

'Do you know of many literary symbols which have not been misunderstood?'

'Of course not.'

'Three Greeks, the writer, the director, the composer, and one American actor, worked together to befog the mind of their readers and viewers.'

She is about to tell me.

'What did they see in the Zorba dance from the film? They saw an affirmation of life, the vital euphoria, the victory over pessimism. What do I see? The inarticulate scream of despair, the masked representation of a dying existence, the constant emptying of all physical and mental faculties before you drop breathless and unconscious into incomprehensibility.'

'Please explain.'

'The initial slow steps stand for the weak and unstable attempts of a fallen existence struggling to recompose itself. As it grows faster and faster despair and helplessness take over; the dancer is failing, his body betrays him, his connection with the others is lost – then the dance is transformed into an exorcism drawing a magical circle to keep all demonic irregularities away, until he collapses and surrenders and capitulates. His fall embodies the death of language.'

I stand puzzled.

'That's the meaning of Zorba, the meaning of the Greek experience. Not Nietzsche's puerile fairy-tales or Heidegger's exoticized topographies. Dying is what the Zorba dance stands for: we are departing, this is our swan song, farewell reason, so long unreason! We are passing through the gates of wordlessness into the vast expanses of meaninglessness.'

She continues: 'You read theology: we are trapped in our self. We exist from within the reality of *incurvatus in se,* unable to escape, to look around, and feel awe.'

'Plato's cave prisoners all over again.'

'Unable to face the light and the rest, oh yes ... That's us, alright. And we think that freedom is in confusion, disorientation, lawlessness.'

She is talking with immense calm as if such powerful indictments were beautiful, cruel, liberating truths.

'I must go now,' she says. 'We will meet again.'

Only the smoke of her cigarette is left behind. I know that my clothes will smell for weeks.

Hercules, Vasso, the three of us: fallen, failed, forgotten.

Silence. Thinking old melodies, remembering bygone enthusiasms, recalling lost unities. Voices, lights flickering, bright lights, dark luminosities. Commanding whispers: '*Salvage lived reality,*' '*Touch the surfaces,*' '*Everything that is here will be here forever.*' Hercules, is that you? I have a temperature, high fever, probably – that stupid tooth again, always destabilising a precarious balance, my ancient enemies, the sweets of my childhood. Give me sleep or give me aspirin, oops, I have fallen off the bed, or maybe not? As I fall, there is only one, sharp, piercing, bitting, stinging voice: 'You must at last finish *Being and Time* – why are you eating so much chocolate, why?'

Mother standing at the door: 'You are feverish. Drink some tea. It's a good medicine.'

But I couldn't stay in bed. Feverish, confused, angry, I get dressed and I hop on a bus – to the old town. Mother is with her friends drinking their evening coffee and celebrating the great events of television. The bus stops at the traffic lights; now, I see you, Vasso, I look at you clearly, sharply, vividly, as I couldn't before. You are in your natural biosphere, the irrefutable eloquence of human frailty. You are slimmer, with grey hair, more fragile than ever, walking down the street reducing the misery of homeless cats, of stray dogs, of lost causes. I follow you. You have one hundred of them, it is excessive, you know, but it brings a smile to all around you, you make them feel puzzled and confused. They cannot understand why you are doing things that cannot be seen and be recognised, that you don't ask for money from any organisation, that you do it out of generosity and a sense of cosmic balance. I see you amongst abandoned factories, vulgar night clubs, dirty streets, noisy old cars, ugly people, ugly traumatised souls – you are there.

Presence. Thanks to you there are no ruins in this country any more.

Day 30

The morning ritual. Drinking instant coffee. I want to inflict pain upon myself. The unreality of reliving things past throws you in the horrible prison of mindless conformism. Talk about others: you exist because they reserve space for you.

It seems that I forget my own principles.

Vasso will be coming later. Soft weather, warm and friendly. What I am doing today? Mr Nicko comes in. He is smoking. He has his charming green hat on. If there was an originary being for modernity, it is this proletarian. The veiled creator and the unveiled creature, simultaneously. He suffers from cancer for the last ten years. They were preparing his funeral; but he is still up and about and the grave is rented to others.

'On Monday,' he announces after he lights his aromatic cigarette, 'I will be going to hospital. You would be gone by then. It seems that dialysis is inevitable – cancer is down, kidney infections are up. This body has been very unsympathetic to me.'

He takes a deep breath.

'Can I tell you one certain thing about my childhood? You like listening and it seems that you are at peace with yourself. May I?'

'Yes, of course.'

'As a child,' he says, 'I used to roam the western parts of the city, when there were no buildings. Only open fields, rocks, bushes, caves and nothing else. I was almost seven when the Germans arrived. They took everything and we had to run after their trucks to steal food or pick up anything that fell off. We were starving. The Germans were laughing; sometimes they threw pieces of food from their trucks to us as if we were animals.'

With his left hand he beats his chest ... His primeval gesture makes me uneasy.

'I haven't forgotten to this day,' he continues with a broken voice, 'how they killed my little friend Sabethai.'

He struggles to regain its composure. He starts again.

'We used to sell water together; we found it in clean wells and remote springs. He was small and we called him Zambo. We worked for a nasty man during the occupation but he gave us some money or food – and that was enough then. Zambo and I walked down towards the centre of Piraeus dragging tin buckets with water on a donkey cart. It was September 1943, when suddenly a German car stopped. Two soldiers with huge guns came out and started looking at his face. His curly hair, his nose, his skin; they finally dragged his pants down. They started yelling, some words which later the boss told me that they meant

Jew. They were abusing him and pushed him towards the back side of their truck. Zambo started fighting, yelling, crying and escaped running towards the open fields of Perama. The soldiers started shooting; he fell on the ground. I went close to him, he grabbed my hand, blood everywhere. 'Nicko, Nicko, hold me, hold me, I feel cold...' Silence. Blood out of his mouth.'

He wipes his tears.

'I have never forgotten the touch of his hand ... I have never forgotten his mother, in a poor house in Perama. Poverty, hunger, misery, our common bonds. I have to go now ... I start feeling the cold myself. Find some place in your mind for the story of my friend, the little Sabethai. It has devoured my heart for over sixty years ... His skinny body, his dark eyes, the blood out of his mouth ... And I am still alive, sick and alive. But the cold is coming closer and closer, at last. We will meet again, me and Zambo. Over the last sixty years there was no single day without him visiting my mind, my dreams, my life. Find some place for him in what you write.'

He walks out like Milton's fallen angel; proud, broken and inarticulate.

My final hours here; ten thirty in the morning. After his story, I get up struggling against immense dysphoria. Two aspirins help for several hours: aspirins, aspirins, give more aspirins. Time starts slowing down. Still looking for the word and the sentence. I hate my own quest. Vasso comes in. She chooses the right timing.

'Give me some ideas,' I implore, 'to heal me and keep me awake. During these weeks I have plunged into an abysmally foreign country, and cannot find my way out.'

She says: 'I have no time for your emotional and intellectual entanglements. This country is always your country. It raised you, it created you, it ascribed an identity to you. It even gave you something more important: the strength to negate and denounce it.'

'Why do I remember it differently?' I ask.

'Because of your expectations, your assumptions, your certainties.'

And without waiting for my response, she says:

'De-creation. Are you aware of this concept by Simone Weil? This is what our experience has been about. This is what Greek history has been about.'

'Tell me more,' I beg.

'Having built a society on pseudo-identities, the only reason for being here is self-annihilation. We live only to survive and subsist – nothing else. No vertical dimension, no horizon, no need for revaluation, no prophetic strength, no imagination to face reality. The process of animalisation has not been transcended, the objective of humanisation hasn't been conceptualised.'

'And what is *de-creation?*

'The inability to visualise completeness. We build everything on the basis of what is missing, not on what is at hand.'

'Where can we see this?'

'It is so obvious that it barely gets noticed. Everything around us is either broken, or fragmented, or left incomplete. Anything outside the small circle of our experiences becomes dangerous, demonic, threatening. We have betrayed everything, we have fallen short of our self – this is the original sin of this society.'

'That's true. We haven't been able to bring anything to its fruition. We have venerated the narcissism of innocence...'

'This led to another characteristic of our society, our internalised helplessness.'

'I know what you mean,' I reply. 'And I know how hard it is to admit it. It is as if somebody cuts your heart into pieces and simultaneously ridicules your inability to react.'

'Since the first day at school, all citizens learn to feel humiliated, or learn to accept that they cannot do anything to change themselves. Then, when crises come, they are all prepared to be victims. Resentful of our betters, we cannot learn and return to a prelinguistic rage.'

She stops and hesitates.

'I know your classicist fantasies about Greece and harmony and order and reason. *The Acropolis is the symbol of modern Greek hell, the burial ground of all contemporary Greek sensitivity.*'

She looks straight into my eyes.

'Remember of Le Corbusier's "*terrible machine that pulverises and dominates*"? His idea that with the Parthenon '*the spirit of power triumphs*"? Only architects can understand the intellectual and emotional desolation caused by buildings.'

She stops again: 'Probably the right word would have been *mis-creation,* the tendency in all of us to disfigure every thing complete. Isn't this the history of the Parthenon?'

'Yes,' she repeats, as if trying to convince herself. 'We desire to deform everything that some manage to create. Our life's purpose is to distort completeness: completeness disturbs the mind of all those who consented to live with mortal lies. We falsify reality, everything true becomes a thorn in our flesh, everything untrue a liberating act of self-assertion.'

'But why?'

'It is the resentment of the epigones against the creations of their ancestors. We admire their works and abandon them in an isolating uniqueness. Our identity is founded on disfigurement and defacement. Every living face becomes the mirror we want to destroy.'

She lights a cigarette and moves towards the door.

'We have been here before,' she laughs at me. 'Your motherland does not want you back. Stay where you are. Even if you come back, you will never return – and as for us here, we have the right to remain premodern, unindividuated, ritualistic. It is our duty to be false. Good day.'

As she leaves Mother comes in:

'She looks pretty distressed. What did you tell her? You have the dreadful tendency to upset those who love you!'

And out I am. My steps bring me to an abandoned factory in Piraeus – but why? It used to make cigarettes for decades but not anymore. Now it lies empty, without human voices, or human presence yet full of traces of a bustling and noisy and unrelenting past. Now, the machines rest idle, the old equipment broken and dusty, the old administration offices untouched for decades, decay, dust and disrepair prevail – cats, dogs and pigeons have made this industrial paradise their dwelling.

At a corner a huge old clock hanging close to the ceiling is still ticking. Why am I here? Is it because when you were young, you passed by with your sister and you were singing and the long corridors of the building echoed and multiplied and magnified your silly youthful songs? Have you forgotten it? It was the first time you heard your voice talking back to you. And your sister's voice too but altered, transfigured, different. If absence responds, then it's time to disappear. Bring the circle to its close.

It is late at night. We sit next to each other – no one is to visit us. It is just us, watching television, the horrible Greek television, its venomous language, its serpentine disorientation, its malignant unreality.

She knows: *'You horrible skunks, you filthy scumbags, you crooks!'*

The Orphic hymn is repeated over and over again; soon I gradually feel like zoning out towards the areas of between and the regions of twilight. I can hear the sound of her voice even as I am plunging into poetic slumber – the beginning of lucid vision starts being crystallized around me. It envelops me with its magnetic aura, its ecstatic luminescence, and singular simplicity.

'Rest,' says she, 'tranquillity can never be given to us in this world.'

But who says that? In which world? To whom?

Mrs Felicity's last stories. We are not watching any shows. We are simply talking.

The earthquake in eighty one: 'The mountains were dancing like waves.' The suicide of an elderly man in eighty six: 'He jumped from the third floor, although some rumours have it that his daughter pushed him to get the inheritance.' The murder of the lonely elderly woman in ninety seven: 'Just for five thousand drachmas. They arrested two Albanians later.' The disappearance of Mrs Maria's son with a married woman, in two thousand and five: 'Probably killed and buried by her husband.' The gender change of Mrs Urania's son in two thousand and eight: 'Such a beautiful man, blond, tall and sexy – and became a woman ... what a waste!' The son of George, from next door, half Chinese, half Greek, a junky: 'As his father was struggling to keep him in the house, he stabbed him and ran away.' The daughter of the same George: 'A nuclear physicist with NASA in the States. Do you see what comes out of the same family?' The inexcusable words that Mrs Zoe said when your brother died: 'How can we forgive her?' The death of an Albanian immigrant last year: 'One hundred people were mourning him with strange lamentations all night long – they said that he was a religious leader in his country.' The discovery of a precious painting at the basement of a poor old man last year: 'He sold it for fifty thousand euros! It was French! How did it end up in his basement in Piraeus?' The fire that destroyed Mrs Georgina's home in which a talking parrot was burnt alive: 'You should have heard the way the parrot screamed! 'Georgina, Georgina, your friend is going...' We were all very sad, is if we lost a child.'

We go on for hours. She gives me all these stories as gifts. This is not a working class area any more – these are the ninety one volumes of *La Comédie Humaine* by Honoré de Balzac. And we have just started: *The Splendour and the Misery of the Working Class,* volume three, chapter nineteen, page three hundred and twenty two, revised edition.

It is already eleven; I want to go to bed. Mrs Felicity is about to leave: 'Time for rest,' she says. She opens the door but then a mild earthquake strikes; we are rattled and shaken, some glasses fall on the floor and break.

'Here we go again,' Mrs Felicity says. 'We will go either through starvation by the state or by natural catastrophe.'

The earthquake returns. We are shaking but we are laughing.

'Hold onto the television set,' Mother shouts. 'What will happen to us, if it falls down and breaks?'

My prayer:

> *Country of blasphemous ruins,*
> *Greece sad relic,*
> *reducing your biography to biology,*
> *choosing to be unstoried,*
> *dismembering your presence,*
> *Gothic Abendland, pre-Homeric,*
> *zoomorphic, hybrid ineffability–*
> *Noisy society of silence.*

Last Day

Sunday morning. Farewell old country. The taxi arrives. I had thirty days of omnipotent Hellenism. Let's hope that they left me unharmed. Primitive political system, tribal society, predatory oligarchy, cannibalistic priestcraft – they all constitute the essential parameters of the failed Neo-Hellenic nationhood. If you are fed with poison, you never become immune to it – you simply become poisonous yourself.

Maybe only these words of this wall graffito, the most political koan I have ever read, stand out:

> *'Our grandfathers, refugees*
> *our parents, immigrants*
> *and today, we are racists.'*

The graffito expresses succinctly the dislocations in a society that chose the infantilism of hallucinogenic extravaganzas, the narcissism of unrealisable projects, the resentment for someone else's success. This lack of agency, creativity and self-reflection left everything spiritless – which led to the fading away of civil society and then to the death of the political, the rise of the de-historicized, of the dystopian, of the nihilistic. And that's where we are at the moment: nihilists in spite of ourselves.

The taxi is here. Departure, midday. Farewell. Mother is crying.

'Come back soon...' she sighs. Kisses, kisses and more kisses, but the driver is in a hurry:

'Let's go,' he shouts. 'The bloody farmers have blocked the streets again since Friday; we must take the long way. Some of us have to work, you know...'

'Let's go fast then,' I say. 'Let's escape the demons of Athens.'

'That's a nice turn of phrase,' he says. And then: 'We are the Demons of Athens, my friend, unfortunately, all of us are the Demons of Athens.'

The saving grace of knowing.

These are my reports from the days of the Great Devastation.

Made in United States
North Haven, CT
05 November 2026

21766920R00154